Supervising Student Teachers the Professional Way

SUPERVISING STUDENT TEACHERS
THE PROFESSIONAL WAY

A Guide for Cooperating Teachers

by

Marvin A. Henry, Ed.D.
Professor of Education
Indiana State University

and

W. Wayne Beasley, Ed.D.
Associate Professor of Education
University of South Florida

Sycamore Press
Terre Haute, Indiana

Library of Congress Catalog Card No. 74-184494

Copyright 1972 by Sycamore Press, P.O. Box 552, Terre Haute, Indiana 47808.

Seventh Printing May, 1975

To the Numerous Student Teachers
Who Have Meandered Throughout These Pages:

May your journey have helped create a straighter path for those who are following you into the profession

MAH
WWB

PREFACE

There is no other sequence of study in teacher preparation which has a more profound impact upon a college student than the experience of student teaching. It is almost universally advocated by critics and friends of education alike as a necessary process for teacher certification, and its practice is virtually unquestioned. One authority has stated that a student undergoes greater personality change during his student teaching experience than at any other equivalent period of time in his life. In a few short weeks he moves from college student to beginning teacher, acquiring a whole new set of skills, attitudes, and responsibilities. This drama of change and development does not unfold on the college campus but takes place in our elementary and secondary schools under the primary direction of a public school teacher. The basic action is realized in the classroom and the supervising teacher is the key to the developmental process.

There are two basic dimensions of the student teaching act. The first is the interpersonal/social dimension - the relationship between the student teacher, supervising teacher, other professional personnel, and classroom pupils. This dimension involves interaction with the student teacher on an emotional and social basis. Attitudes, values, and feelings permeate the entire relationship. The second dimension involves the process of instruction. The student teacher must learn the basic procedures of determining instructional content and developing successful teaching strategies. Both the personal and the instructional dimensions are necessary for a successful experience and one cannot be completely separated from the other. The supervising teacher is in the vital position of determining the basic pattern for these two dimensions.

This book is designed to assist the supervising teacher in responding to the responsibilities of working with a student teacher. It attempts to provide basic guidelines for employment in the complex process of supervision. It is premised on the belief that effective supervision is accomplished when the supervising teacher makes a decision in the context of a specific need instead of attempting to apply an arbitrary rule which has to be followed regardless of the exigency of the immediate environment. This document should be of prime value for the beginning supervising teacher, but experienced supervisors should also find it useful as a supplementary resource. It is also designed to serve as a text for college courses in techniques of supervising student teachers. Public school administrators and college supervisors should find it a useful reference for overseeing student teaching programs. The student teacher can find these pages to be a revealing background for understanding the new environment which he will soon experience.

The content of this book was created from questions which were asked by supervising teachers at professional meetings, courses in techniques of supervising student teachers, and during individual conferences with the authors. The consolidation of these questions formulated the basic organizational structure. The content is designed to react to these concerns in a systematic fashion, and it attempts to provide guidelines which will assist the individual supervising teacher in his decision making.

Each chapter, and each section within a chapter, is written so that it may be considered independently according to the interests or needs of the reader. The first chapter deals with the initial topics that a potential supervising teacher may want to know about in preparing for a student teacher. Subsequent chapters present the normal activities and processes of a typical student teaching experience, if there is such a composite. The concluding chapter deals with evaluation, the final formal activity of the supervising teacher. One chapter, "Supervising the Problem Student Teacher," describes some of the most-frequently experienced supervisory problems and suggests alternative procedures for dealing with those difficulties. It is written for the more unusual situations whereas the rest of the chapters treat the more typical responsibilities.

Each chapter is initiated with an anecdote which is designed to identify a supervisory concern related to the content of that section. The narration which follows attempts to briefly summarize the major principles and ideas which have been identified through professional research and theory. Extensive use is made of lists which can be quickly studied by the teacher who is seeking answers to a specific question. Case studies are designed to focus on individualized problems of student teaching, and alternatives are provided for consideration and discussion. No attempt is made to imply a correct "solution," because the real course of action depends on many factors relevant to the immediate situation. Hopefully, an understanding of such problems will help the supervising teacher prevent their occurrence. Worksheets are provided throughout the book in order to give the teacher a few concrete supervisory tools.

Each chapter closes with an anecdote which implies possible solution to the problem identified initially in the chapter. A summary set of principles is stated to reiterate briefly the major ideas in the chapter. References are then provided for those who wish to pursue a particular topic in greater detail.

This book could not have become a reality without the assistance and cooperation of a great number of people. The most important group, undoubtedly, was that number of teachers who provided the questions which formulated the basic outline for its contents. The authors are indebted, as well, to members of their classes in techniques of supervising student teachers who read the manuscript and suggested revisions which would make the content more appropriate for supervising teachers. One such class member, Delmar Miller, a staff member at Ben

Davis High School, Indianapolis, Indiana, must be recognized for his thorough and perceptive reaction to the manuscript from a teacher's point of view.

Special recognition is due to Dr. Curtis Nash, Dean of the School of Education at Central Michigan University, Dr. Alan Quick, Director of Student Teaching at Central Michigan, Dr. Jarvis Wotring, university supervisor at the same institution, and Dr. Ray Phillips, Coordinator of Laboratory Experiences at Auburn University, who read the entire manuscript and offered constructive reactions from their respective positions. We are particularly indebted to Dr. William Van Til, Lotus D. Coffman Distinguished Professor of Education at Indiana State University, for his insight, analysis and encouragement in the early stages of the preparation of the manuscript. The writers, and the readers as well, must offer much appreciation to Jane Angell who read an early copy of the manuscript, and offered several suggestions concerning the writing style.

If this publication has provided a set of guidelines which will cause the complex task of supervision of student teachers to be executed more efficiently, we will have achieved our task. If this be the case, we should be one step further toward attaining the goal of cooperatively preparing better teachers for the schools of tomorrow.

MAH
WWB

CONTENTS

WORKSHEETS

Worksheet

CASE STUDIES

Chapter One

BEFORE THE STUDENT TEACHER ARRIVES

Elaine Bennett made a routine stop at her mail box and discovered a note from Mr. Williams, the principal, requesting that she see him at her convenience. When she had the opportunity to inquire about the message, she was informed that State University would like to place a student teacher in the school next semester. Mr. Williams asked Miss Bennett if she would consent to be the supervisor since the student was particularly qualified to work in her area of specialization. Miss Bennett expressed reservations about accepting the task because she felt unprepared for this new role, but when Mr. Williams assured her that he was confident that she had the potential for being a good supervisor, she reluctantly agreed.

Mr. Williams handed her a student-teacher information form to look over and suggested that she talk to some of the other cooperating teachers in the building in order to learn something about the university requirements for student teaching. The information sheets indicated that the student teacher would probably spend a few days visiting the school prior to the start of the actual experience. She only hoped that she could learn something very quickly about supervising a student teacher.

A few days later, Brian Sims, a senior at State University, moves through a long line of students who are awaiting the distribution of their student teaching assignments. A secretary hands him a standardized form, and he stares at its contents. With a puzzled look on his face, he turns to a friend and inquires, "Do you know anything about Central City?"

Brian is directed to a group meeting where a college supervisor provides a sketchy description of student teaching and concludes by stressing the value of a pre-student-teaching visit in order to become familiar with the environment where they will be completing their professional work. He emphasizes the necessity of planning a teaching schedule and of learning as much about the school as possible. The students are informed that further details about student teaching will become apparent as they meet their supervising teachers.

Brian begins to make preparation for his visit by writing to Miss Bennett, indicating when he plans to make his pre-teaching contact. In his letter, he raises several questions about teaching and states that he is anxious to learn more about his responsibilities, the community, the school, and the pupils. . .

A STUDENT TEACHER IS COMING: Anxious Anticipation

A student teaching experience actually begins for the supervising teacher and the student teacher the moment they are notified of the assignment. Each must now begin to make preparation for this activity which will bring them together as co-workers. The student will need to arrange to visit the school where he is assigned to student-teach so that he may become familiar with the actual teaching environment. The cooperating teacher has to learn about the university's student teaching program and to prepare his pupils for the new situation caused by the presence of a college student who will be assuming a teacher's role. Both are aware that some adjustments in routine will be necessary, and each may experience some anxiety as he begins to make preparation for the new working relationship.

The nature of pre-student-teaching contacts can either set the stage for a worthwhile student teaching experience or create an uneasy atmosphere which could pervade the entire period of professional experience. Consider the apprehension of a student teacher who writes a letter of introduction to the school or teacher and either receives no reply or a belated, indifferent response. On the other hand, consider the reservations which could develop in the mind of a supervising teacher who receives no advance communication or information regarding his student teacher. Many questions can be answered and potential misunderstandings can be thwarted if communication is established early. The student teacher usually initiates correspondence, and his designated supervisor can help the student teacher look forward to the assignment if he makes a prompt and warm response. Before student teaching actually begins, the supervising teacher can assist in establishing a rapport between himself and the student teacher.

A great deal of preparation will probably be necessary before any additional information is made available. In most situations there will be no further communication from the university until the student teacher has arrived to begin his work. Effective preparation includes knowing something of the requirements of a student teaching program, making adjustments to allow for participation by a student teacher, and developing the concept of working on a team basis with a teaching candidate.

The supervising teacher will have to be prepared to modify his teaching style to assimilate a new personality into the classroom routine. The individuality of a student teacher is a variable that can determine the types of responsibilities he will assume as well as when he will assume them. The confident, outgoing student may be able to adjust to most situations, but the timid or insecure person may need responsibilities which build confidence. Better initial procedures for the experience can be provided if attention is paid to assessment of personality in early contacts.

Grade-point averages earned by a student in his college classes are not always accurate predictors of his knowledge or potential teaching skill. Many college classes place a priority on recall, and items which have been memorized for a test may be either irrelevant to the public school classroom or forgotten prior to their actual need. On the other hand, it cannot be assumed that student teachers with low scholastic averages are potentially better teachers or have a more practical knowledge of content. There seems to be little or no correlation. Students at all levels along the index continuum may be good, average, or poor in regard to actual subject knowledge or teaching skill required for student teaching.

A fact of educational practice seems to be that one teaches not by how he was taught to teach but by how he was actually taught. College students for the most part have been overexposed to the lecture method of instruction with emphasis on covering content. Classes in professional education may have closely resembled the style of academic classes. Even if such techniques were different, the student with his lack of experience may have considered any unfamiliar procedure to be either unrealistic or impractical. It is entirely possible that the student teacher may conceive of teaching as nothing more than presiding at an "intellectual soup kitchen" where a bit of knowledge is doled out in quantities by someone standing in front of the room.

One of the major tasks of the student teacher is the development of adequate concepts of good teaching. No course work can completely insure that the student fully understands the vital processes of pedagogy. Initially, for instance, he may feel that advance planning is a chore dreamed up by a theoretical methods professor. His concept of individual differences may be extremely remote, and he may define discussion as retrieving rote answers from the textbook. There has been little opportunity for him to acquire skill in the techniques of communication or effective utilization of media. The idea of student involvement and activity may be frightening, and he may wish to avoid it if at all possible. Only the proper guided experience will result in maximum development in acquiring proficiency in these teaching processes.

The objective of a professional certification program is to prepare a candidate to assume full classroom responsibility by having acquired certain teaching skills through selected studies and guided participation. Student teaching is designed to give a teaching candidate who has acquired such knowledge the experience of teaching under the supervision of a master teacher.

Student teaching was created on the premise that experience is vital in the process of complete professionalization of a teacher. Competency in this professional skill is impossible without supervised activity. In the developmental stages performance of the act alone is not sufficient. If learning is to occur, the participant must reflect on the nature of his experience, analyze what he has done, and plan for a future course of action. In other words, doing something is not in itself enough, but it is essential in teaching development. The function of a student teaching program is to structure an environment in which the teaching candidate can actually attempt to direct learning, to reflect upon his experience with the assistance of other professionals, and to develop patterns of behavior which will make him more successful in guiding learning experiences for others.

Student teaching rests on a base of preparation in general education, proficiency in an area of specialization, acquaintance with educational principles, and a little association with pupils in a learning environment. Through the process of guided activity, the student teacher launches into his own orbit--the ability to function effectively in the world of the first-year teacher. The course will be determined by the experience of student teaching.

AN EMOTIONAL EXPERIENCE: **From Exhilaration to Despondency in One Easy (or One Difficult) Lesson**

Student teaching is an emotional experience for the teaching candidate because of its nature, importance, and potential impact upon his career. It is the apex of the college years, testing the ability to perform that task which has been the goal for nearly four years and which is potentially his future livelihood. He will probably have a more inadequate concept of his potential for success in student teaching than he has had for most of his classes in college. In addition, he may be entering a new community or a new school as a complete stranger. His thoughts prior to student teaching will turn to such anxieties as what the supervising teacher will expect of him, whether he will be able to establish a teacher's bearing in the presence of pupils, whether he can manage a classroom, and whether his academic preparation is adequate.

Student teaching is a new and different life for most college students. This newness can initiate an emotional cycle which runs from elation to dejection. Researchers have discovered that this "innovation cycle" seems to be typical of any new experience. It involves different levels of emotional reaction at various stages in the period of development involved. A typical eight-week student teaching experience indicates the following emotional cycle:[1]

WEEKS

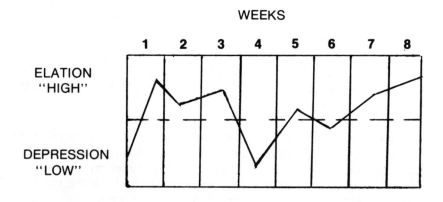

The student enters the experience insecure and fearful. He is likely to feel a combination of curiosity, hope, and anxiety. These initial fears are soon allayed as he is welcomed by the staff and finds that the pupils are really human after all. He may reach his peak of enthusiasm after a few days as a student teacher. Typically, a rather sharp decline to a state of depression will occur in about the third or fourth week. This may

[1]Donald M. Sharpe, **A Brief Guide to Secondary Student Teaching,** Indiana State University, Terre Haute, Indiana, 1970, p. 11.

be caused by such factors as an altercation with a pupil, poor grades on the first test he gives, or a criticism by the supervising teacher. After this low, he should gradually build to a greater feeling of confidence and maturity, feeling generally optimistic or satisfied with his progress at the conclusion of the period. This indescribable metamorphosis--learning to handle one's uncomfortable feelings in the complex, unpredictable situations which arise in human relations and in the classroom, learning to apply general principles and to formulate original principles and check them against the experience of mature members of the profession--is one of the most important contributions of supervised teaching.[2]

PROBLEMS OF STUDENT TEACHERS: **Technical Flaws in the Countdown**

Nearly every student teacher will experience problems to some degree. A realization of this fact makes the adjustment easier for both student teacher and supervisor. Most problems are related to instructional techniques and pupil control and guidance. Student teachers may tend to be more superficial in their assessments of some difficulties than supervising teachers, and they may tend to attribute the causes of these dilemmas to others. Student teachers are inclined to experience most intensely those difficulties related to deficiencies in general teaching personality, such as lack of confidence and lack of dynamic qualities in the classroom. These problems are more severe when experienced, but they are not as likely to occur as those related to instructional techniques and pupil control.

Research on problems of student teachers seems to show that personality problems are the most serious problems faced by the student teachers, but the supervising teachers are more likely to be concerned with difficulties related to instruction. These studies indicate that supervising teachers and student teachers are inclined to agree on the types of difficulties experienced, although supervising teachers put less emphasis on the more trivial problems. Communication concerning the nature of the problem usually is not difficult in most situations.[3]

The summary below indicates the types of difficulties which are most frequently experienced by student teachers. The degree of intensity, of course, varies with each student.

2**Ibid**., p. 11.

3 Marvin A. Henry, **The Relationship of Difficulties of Student Teachers to Selected Aspects of the Professional Sequence of Education.** Unpublished Doctor's Thesis, Indiana University, Bloomington, 1963.

Pupil control and discipline
   Eliminating noise and other disturbances
   Pupil animosities
   Securing pupil cooperation
Motivating pupil interest and response
   Procuring and maintaining pupil interest
   Encouraging a wide range of pupil participation
Presenting the lesson and guiding pupil discussion
   Introducing topics
   Adapting explanations to the understanding of pupils
Lack of an effective teaching voice
   Quality of voice
   Tone control
   Use of expression
Lack of dynamic qualities of personality
   Lack of animation, enthusiasm, friendliness, and liveliness
Lack of confidence
   Nervous tension
   Worries
   Symptoms of fear
Planning and organization of learning activities
   Making adequate preparation
   Selecting and organizing subject matter and materials
   Planning teaching procedures
Handling broader aspects of teaching
   Application of general principles and theory in guiding learning
Questioning
   Proper phrasing
   Providing a variety of types of questions
   Directing questions to a small minority in the class
   Calling on pupils before stating questions
   Answering own questions
Budgeting time
Lack of command over subject matter
*Conflict of personal goals and philosophy with that of the school or
   supervising teacher*

PREPARING FOR THE STUDENT TEACHER'S ARRIVAL: **Preliminaries in the Ready Room**

Specific planning for a student teacher's arrival begins with the preparation of the pupils in the classroom, continues through the planning of procedures for introductory activities, and culminates in arrangements for the orientation of the student teacher. Advance planning is as beneficial in preparing for student teacher supervision as it is in preparing to teach a class. Its dimensions are different, but its nature determines the format for the experience.

Preparing the Class

A perceptive teacher will give high priority to the establishment of the student teacher's status with the class before he arrives. The pupils ought to know that a student teacher is coming and should anticipate his arrival with some eagerness. Typical preparation will include:

Creating anticipation that more interesting and worthwhile experiences will be possible
- Cite increased knowledge or skills which a student teacher might possess
- Refer to possible activities that might be achieved while *two* teachers are working with the group
- Make plans for some ambitious projects which could be pursued

Initiating correspondence between the class and the student teacher
- Class members could introduce themselves and explain their work through a letter
- Class members could indicate goals which they hope they can achieve while the student teacher is with them
- Class members might make some requests which would utilize university resources which the student teacher would have available
- The student teacher might be encouraged to write a letter of introduction describing his preparation, interests, and experiences which would be related to the work of the class

Describing the purposes of student teaching
- Differences between regular teaching and student teaching
- Goals and skills which the student teacher should achieve while he is in the school

Explaining how the members of the class can help the student teacher
- Cooperation
- Interest
- Acquaintance with the school and routine
- Formulation of teaching attitudes through interaction with pupils

Professional Preparation

The supervising teacher will need to give considerable attention to the organization of the instructional content and teaching activities which will occur while the student teacher is participating in the class.

The presence of this second teacher can increase the number of activities that could be pursued. The following are usually within the range of possibility:

> *Team teaching*
> *Enrichment activities*
>> *Field trips*
>> *Extensive projects*
> *Utilization of resource material that might be available at the student teacher's university*
> *Experimentation with different techniques*

Preparing the Student Teacher

Nearly all student teachers will have received some orientation to student teaching, but there are certain types of preparation that can only be accomplished by the cooperating school and the supervising teacher. For example, the future student teacher will likely have only a vague, apprehensive concept of what his early activities and responsibilities will be, and he will probably welcome the following information about his new environment:

Information about the location of the school
> *A map of the school and community can be helpful*
Instructions on reporting to the proper personnel upon arrival at the school
Any printed material that he might need or want to study prior to the initial visit
Information about the community in general
Sharing of any ideas about the experience
An invitation to begin considering various topics or ideas which can be discussed during the first visit

The Pre-Teaching Contact

A pre-teaching visit is usually a routine part of student teaching procedure. This visit may occur several days or several weeks in advance of the date for the initiation of the actual experience. Directions for this contact may be highly structured or they can be extremely informal. In either case, it is important to remember that mutual impressions are being formed and that these reactions are very fundamental to future working relationships.

The pre-teaching visit is not a mere formality--it is an intensive work session. The student teacher will want to visit classes and become acquainted with his supervisor. He will need to learn about the school and meet its key personnel. This time will provide the opportunity to discuss and clarify some points of concern which are not clear to either party. The major tasks of this visit are summarized as follows:

Determination of a teaching load for student teaching
Becoming acquainted with instructional materials
Getting to know something about the students
Planning initial teaching activities of the student teacher
Getting to know something about the school and community

Case Study No. 1: THE POTENTIAL STUDENT TEACHER SEEMS INDIFFERENT DURING THE PRE-TEACHING VISIT

The first visit by your student teacher did not develop as you had anticipated. He seemed to be bored and indifferent instead of appearing excited and inquisitive as you had hoped. He did not seem to follow the discussion as evidenced by his looking out the window and by his making no visible signs that he might care about what you are doing. He took little interest in discussion of future plans for his student teaching. He did make a very revealing comment when he stated that he might not teach after graduation because he was not certain that he was really interested in education.

As his future supervising teacher, what course of action do you take?

1. Take no action on the assumption that one cannot expect much interest on a visit of this type
2. Try to arouse his interest in teaching by citing its value in relation to other types of positions
3. Call the university and indicate that you have decided that you cannot accept this student teacher
4. Call the university, describe the incident and seek assistance
5. Attempt to have the student teacher become more directly involved in activity during the visit
6. Suggest that he not stay as long as he had planned
7. Discuss the specific activities which he needs to be thinking about before he returns to student teaching
8. _____

Consider:

a. Types of activities which might prevent a visitor from becoming bored in your classroom
b. Ways of promoting teaching as an exciting activity
c. The nature of your own teaching
d. Analysis of techniques of your own communication with individuals.
e. _____

Case Study No. 2: THE VISITOR IS RELUCTANT TO BECOME INVOLVED IN ACTIVITY

You were expecting that a student teacher would indicate that she had a lot to learn through student teaching, but you were not prepared for what happened during her first visit. She appeared extremely insecure in every situation and confessed that she was not familiar with the subject matter you were teaching since it had been a while since she had taken any course in that area. She was reluctant to participate in any class activities and seemed not to want to become involved in any way. You further observed that she seemed to avoid the pupils as much as possible in the informal moments.

What action should you take?

1. Do nothing at the present since this is the first contact with your class
2. Investigate her record for clues to this kind of behavior
3. Attempt to structure some activity so that she will receive positive reinforcement
4. Give her some materials to study before she returns for student teaching
5. Introduce her to pupils so that she can get to know them as individuals
6. Notify the university of your concerns
7. _____

> *Consider:*
> a. Procedures which will help a person feel confortable in a new surrounding
> b. The dynamics in your teaching area which might encourage uncertainty on the part of a student teacher
> c. _____

INFORMATION ABOUT THE STUDENT TEACHER: **Curiosity Pays**

A fundamental premise in sound educational practice is that a teacher works better with his students if he knows something about them. Most authorities agree that proceeding in ignorance will increase the possibility of making wrong judgments, pursuing ineffective procedures, and following circuitous routes in achieving desired objectives. The supervising teacher needs information about his student teacher in order to guide him in his professional experience.

Much information will be accrued as the student teacher and supervisor work together. This is good and should be encouraged, but it should be built upon a body of information that the teacher has had an opportunity to consider prior to the first contact. Data most commonly sought and usually available are:

Educational background
   Courses taken in major and minor areas

General education
Experiences in working with children or young people
High school performance and activities
General experiences
Employment
Military service
Community service (social service, camps, religious activities,
    recreational supervision)
Leadership responsibilities
Travel
Personal characteristics
Age
Health; physical limitations
Recreational interests; hobbies
Marital status
Family background
Autobiographical statement
Participation in campus activities
Professional goals
Reasons for pursuing those goals

A considerable amount of the desired information is normally summarized by the student when he applies for student teaching. A copy of this resume is usually forwarded by the university to the cooperating school where the student teaching assignment has been requested. If it has not been made available to the supervising teacher, an inquiry to the individual who is charged with the assignment of student teachers in the school will probably reveal its location. If he does not have the information, he will be able to contact the university for such materials.

All information received in written form will need to be supplemented and interpreted through informal conferences with the student teacher and with those who know him at the university. Two considerations need to be stressed in the process of gathering information about a student teacher: (1) Information should be exchanged in an atmosphere of mutual respect, and (2) The student teacher should know why the information is desired. Relevant information openly shared will help both student teacher and supervising teacher better understand each other.

PROVIDING INFORMATION ABOUT THE SCHOOL AND COMMUNITY:
Stranger in the Promised Land

The school environment may be more strange to the student teacher than one would suppose. Since the supervising teacher has probably lived in the community and taught in its school system for some time, he may sometimes assume that the student teacher is also familiar with the school and community. There is a sizable amount of information that will aid the newcomer in understanding the school community, and it will be extremely helpful for the student if the supervisor has considered this prior to the beginning of student teaching. Depending on the individual situation, attention should be called to the following:

Information about the school in general
    Type of population it serves
    Philosophy
    Unique characteristics, facilities, or services
School policies relating to the teachers
School policies relating to the students
Forms and reports which must be completed
Emergency procedures
Specific information about pupils
School schedule of classes
School directory
School calendar
Location of the classroom in relation to the office, work rooms,
   cafeteria, teachers' lounge, rest rooms, and library
Service facilities
    Procedure in getting materials reproduced
    Audio-visual services and resources
    Supplies
Teacher responsibilities in the extracurricular program

There are several methods of acquainting the student teacher with the responsibilities of teachers before he assumes full-time residence as a participant. A school handbook, for instance, is quite beneficial in helping a student teacher understand the school. In the absence of or in addition to this information, some administrators provide orientation programs for prospective student teachers which help acquaint them with the many important facets of the school program. Other faculty members are usually willing to help with initial orientation as well. The pre-teaching visit provides a good opportunity for introductions to teachers who will voluntarily assist the student teacher in getting acquainted with the school.

Community

A community handbook is often available from a local service organization and can be a very useful resource. If one is unavailable, the supervisor may want to describe those facilities which will be necessary or useful to the student teacher. The following list is typical of the student teacher's needs in learning about a new area:

Living accommodations
Restaurants
Available transportation
Recreational facilities and places of interest
Service facilities
Location of shopping areas
Community customs
Community social structure

Case Study No. 3: A STUDENT TEACHER IN NEED OF HOUSING FACILITIES

During your student teacher's initial visit, he says that he does not know where he will be able to live. Since he is not familiar with the community, he has no available contacts. He feels that he has searched "everywhere" and cannot find a place to live and he fears that he might have to commute from the campus which is seventy miles away.
What course of action do you take?

1. Encourage him to drive from campus
2. Try to find a place for him to live
3. Suggest additional sources for contact which may not have occurred to him
4. Ignore the statement and let him work out his own personal details
5. _____

   Consider:

   a. The role of good housing in adjustment to a new environment
   b. How a friendly gesture in finding housing will affect communication between teacher and student teacher
   c. The effect that uncertainities of this type may have upon the initial adjustment of the student teacher to his new role
   d. _____

ETHICAL CONDUCT: Playing the Game by the House Rules

A professional adheres to certain standards because they are dictated by the profession itself. Educators agree that a teacher should conform to the standards of his profession and conduct himself in an ethical manner. Student teaching is not too early to begin operation by the same standards. A student teacher should be aware of such a code and ought to adhere to it. In the event that he is not cognizant of the concept of ethical behavior, the rationale and code can be discussed in an early conference.

A student teacher code of ethics has been developed locally in an instance or two. Some student teachers may have been exposed to a code such as the one listed below:[4]

Student Teacher Code of Ethics

1. All information which the student teacher receives about pupils in his class or school is to be kept confidential.
2. A student teacher should be more concerned with what is being achieved with the pupils than with the impressions being made on the supervising teacher or college supervisor.
3. The student teacher should maintain the dignity necessary to gain the respect of his pupils.
4. The student teacher should show enthusiasm concerning the learning experiences being developed with pupils.
5. The student teacher should be sympathetic and courteous toward all pupils.
6. The student teacher should consider himself a member of the community in which he is teaching and act accordingly.
7. Disciplinary measures used by the student teacher should conform to the instructions of the supervising teacher.
8. The student teacher must be an example to his pupils in every way--physically, mentally, ethically.
9. The student teacher should be just as interested in and be as ready to assist with the improvement of a class as if it were his own.
10. The student teacher must realize that each pupil is an individual, and must take into consideration individual abilities, interests, and capacities for learning.
11. The student teacher must be completely impartial in dealing with pupils, and must constantly strive to be fair while judging pupils' actions.
12. The student teacher should refrain from imposing his religious or political views upon his pupils, and should exhibit a broad-minded, tolerant attitude toward other groups and individuals.

The student teacher code of ethics, of course, is not an absolute standard. Like any code, it will need to be interpreted with the actual experience as the context. If the supervising teacher and the student teacher make a conscious effort to adhere to ethical practice from the beginning, a more responsible teacher will emerge.

4 Sharpe, **op. cit,** p. 24

Worksheet No. 1: A FINAL CHECKLIST FOR PREPARATION FOR A STUDENT TEACHER

Before the student teacher arrives for student teaching, the supervising teacher should:

1. have prepared the pupils for the arrival of the student teacher
2. have learned about the background of the student teacher
3. have read the university student teaching handbook, if one is available, and understand the role of a supervising teacher
4. have become aware of the legal status of student teachers in his state
5. have become familiar with the policy of his school concerning the responsibilities of student teachers
6. have had pre-teaching contact with the student teacher
7. have secured copies of materials that can be used in orienting the student teacher, e.g., school handbook, schedule of classes
8. have made provision for the student teacher to have a desk or table of his own to use
9. have secured copies of teachers' editions of class textbooks and curriculum guides for the student teacher
10. have tentatively planned a balanced sequence of learning experiences for the student teacher for the total student teaching assignment

Brian Sims guided his five-year-old automobile into the faculty parking lot and eased into a slot reserved for visitors. After hastily checking a few papers, he walked quickly to the main entrance of the school and followed the signs to the principal's office.

A few minutes later, there is a knock on Miss Bennett's door. She is greeted by the principal who introduces the new student teacher from State University.

"I would like you to meet Brian Sims, who is here to make his pre-teaching visit."

"Hello, Brian," said Miss Bennett with a sincere smile, "welcome to Central City."

As the principal returned to the office, Miss Bennett and Brian moved into the classroom.

"I'm glad you are here," began Miss Bennett," I hope we can make some plans for your teaching, and I would like to know something of your particular interests. I also want to show you the school so that you will know about our facilities before you begin student teaching."

"I appreciate this opportunity," replied the more-relaxed visitor. "I still have several questions about my responsibilities, and I would like to know about your students so that I can make some plans while I have university resources available."

The conversation continued until late in the afternoon. Brian was seen leaving the building with a stack of books and papers. His small car moved smoothly out of the parking lot, apparently headed for a quick look at the downtown area before returning to the campus.

Remember:

More anxiety may occur prior to student teaching than during the actual experience

Little information about the school or the supervising teacher is provided for the student teacher before his first contact with the school

Three factors are important in determining the effectiveness of pre-student-teaching experiences:

The degree of student readiness for such participation

The quality of teacher guidance

The type of school and community

The teacher sets the classroom atmosphere and activity structure before the student teacher arrives

The best orientation plans are designed to cause the student to feel that he is to be a definite part of the school and community

Student teaching is a period of transition in which the teaching candidate changes from college student to beginning teacher

Student teaching is a process, not an end product

USEFUL REFERENCES

ASSOCIATION FOR STUDENT TEACHING. *Guiding Student Teaching Experiences,* The Association for Student Teaching, Bulletin No. 1, 1969, pp. 1-2, 8.
Values of student teaching
Preparing for the arrival of a student teacher

ASSOCIATION FOR STUDENT TEACHING, *New Developments, Research, and Experimentation in Professional Laboratory Experiences,* The Association for Student Teaching, Bulletin No. 22, 1964, pp. 129-30, 136, 138-139.
Experiences which should be provided for student teachers
Pre-teaching visit

ASSOCIATION FOR STUDENT TEACHING, *Professional Growth Inservice of the Supervising Teacher,* The Association for Student Teaching, Forty-fifth Year-book, 1966, Chapter 2.
Problems of student teachers

ASSOCIATION FOR STUDENT TEACHING, *A Theoretical Basis for Professional Laboratory Experiences in Teacher Education,* The Association for Student Teaching, 1966.
Rationale for student teaching

BLAIR, LOIS, "Are You Good Enough to be a Supervising Teacher?" *Teachers College Journal* 32:25-29, 45-46, October, 1960.
Criteria in considering the qualifications of supervising teachers

BLASER, FRANK, AND McEWIN, TOM, "Student Teachers Strengthen your Schools," *ISBA Journal* 16:5, May, 1970, pp. 3-4.
Contributions of the student teacher to the school

CURTIS, DWIGHT, AND ANDREWS, L. O., *Guiding Your Student Teacher,* New York: Prentice-Hall, 1954, Chapters 1-3.
What is student teaching
Teacher's functions in guiding student teachers

Desirable competencies for supervising teachers
Effect of student teaching upon pupils
Securing information about the student teacher
Acquainting the student teacher with the school
Planning a tentative program with the student teacher
Planning to acquaint the student with the community

DALE, R. S., "You have a Student Teacher? Relax!" *Business Education World* 48:7-9, January, 1968.
    Anticipating a student teacher

HENRY, MARVIN A., *The Relationship of Difficulties of Student Teachers to Selected Aspects of the Professional Sequence of Education,* Unpublished Doctoral Dissertation, Indiana University, Bloomington, Indiana, 1963.
    Problems of student teachers

HENRY, MARVIN A., "Supervising Teachers Report Attitudes Concerning Selected Aspects of Student Teaching," *Supervisors Quarterly* 6:3, Spring, 1971, pp 33-36.
    Reports of surveys distributed to cooperating teachers

HUNTER, ELIZABETH AND AMIDON, EDMUND, *Student Teaching,* The Odyssey Press, New York, 1964.
    Worries of student teachers

INDIANA STATE DEPARTMENT OF PUBLIC INSTRUCTION, *The Hoosier Schoolmaster of the Sixties* 7:1, September, 1967.
    Rationale for student teaching
    Goals of student teaching
    Cooperative partnerships
    Responsibilities of a school system

KLEIN, JACOB, "The Role of the Classroom Teacher in Teacher Preparation," *North Dakota Teacher* 44:9-12, February, 1965.
    Responsibilities of the supervising teacher

KRAFT, LEONARD, "You're Getting a Student Teacher," *The National Elementary Principal,* January, 1966, pp. 17-18.
    Before the student teacher arrives

NELSON, DALE E., "What Both Parties Should Remember," *Business Education World* 48:9-10, January, 1968.
    Orientation to student teaching
    What a supervisor should expect from his student teacher

ROTH, LOIS H., "Selecting Supervising Teachers," *The Journal of Teacher Education* 12:476-481, December, 1961.
    Characteristics of effective supervisors

SHARPE, DONALD M., *A Brief Guide to Secondary Student Teaching,* Indiana State University, Terre Haute, 1970.
    Orientation to student teaching

SLEEPER, WILLIAM R., AND TELFER, HAROLD E., "Planning Orientation to Student-Teaching." *The Journal of Teacher Education* 13:50-54, March, 1962.
    Preparing for the student teacher

SORENSON, G., AND HALPERT, R. "Stress in Student Teaching," *California Journal of Educational Research,* 19:28-33, January, 1968.
    Problems of student teachers

STEEVES, FRANK, *Issues in Student Teaching.* The Odyssey Press, Inc., New York, 1963, Chapter 3.
    Information about student teachers

STRATEMEYER, FLORENCE B., AND LINDSEY, MARGARET, *Working With Student Teachers,* Teachers College Press, Columbia University, New York, 1958, pp. 127-151.

What needs to be known prior to beginning student teaching

TANRUTHER, EDGAR M., *Clinical Experiences in Teaching for the Student Teacher or Intern,* Dodd, Mead and Company, New York, 1967, Chapter 1.

Planning for student teaching

Getting acquainted with school and community

Teacher development team

TAYLOR, GEM KATE, "Factors in the Decision to become a Supervising Teacher," *Peabody Journal of Education,* 38:351-352, May, 1961.

Factors for consideration in the decision to accept a student teacher

THOMPSON, MICHAEL, "Identifying Anxieties Experienced by Student Teachers," *The Journal of Teacher Education* 14:435-439, December, 1963.

Student teacher anxieties

TRENFIELD, WILLIAM, "Your Student Teacher: An Asset in the Classroom?" *Supervisors Quarterly* 6:2, pp 35-39, Winter 70-71.

Contributions of a student teacher

TRIPLETT, D., "Student Teachers Rank Their Needs," *Michigan Education Journal* 45:13-14, November, 1967.

Aspects of the teaching act that are of most concern to student teachers

Chapter Two

INTRODUCING THE STUDENT TO TEACHING

Brian Sims arrived early at the school on his first day of student teaching. The secretary indicated that he could go directly to Miss Bennett's room since Mr. Williams, the principal, was busy and would not be able to see him until later. Making his way down the hall, he arrived at Miss Bennett's room just as she entered carrying a stack of papers. After the initial greetings, they made small talk as they waited for the school day to begin.

Brian attempted to appear to be at ease, but he could not conceal his tensions. All the requirements given him last week in orientation at the university seemed to whirl around in his head as the school emitted the sounds of a busy Monday morning. Appearance! Requirements! Ethics! Teaching! Observations! Planning! Organization! Student behavior! In a way the orientation instructions seemed more remote and abstract as the actual situation was realized in an authentic school environment. He asked a few hurried questions and, almost as an afterthought, mentioned that a college supervisor would be around to visit soon to acquaint Miss Bennett with the college program of student teaching. He clenched the arm of his chair as the minute hand pointed to the top of the hour.

The complexity of the supervisory task became more apparent to Miss Bennett as she talked with her beginning student teacher. So much was at stake for him. She was a little uneasy herself since this was a new experience for her. Many details had to be attended to quickly, but the first task which had to be performed, obviously, was to acquaint class and student teacher. The bell sounded and attendance was quickly checked. She arose from her desk more carefully than usual, cleared her throat, looked at her pupils, and began to introduce her first student teacher to the class . . .

THE FIRST FEW DAYS: **Adjustment, Learning, and Demands**

The arrival of a student teacher interjects a new dimension into the classroom environment which is sensed by both pupils and teacher. Anticipation and correspondence can cause limited preparedness for the impending change, but only the physical presence of the student teacher in the classroom provides the full impact of this different educational climate. The student teacher is confronted with a whole new series of tasks which may cause him to be apprehensive and rather awkward in the classroom in spite of his best efforts to appear relaxed.

The first few days are periods of adjustment and learning. If the first experiences of a student teacher are successful, subsequent responsibilities will pose much less threat. During these initial days, the student teacher has a number of tasks to meet:

He must become acquainted with the school and its personnel
He has to get to know his students
He needs to familiarize himself with the classroom routine
He frequently has to arrange for living accommodations
He will begin to assume some responsibility for teaching

Failure or delay in achieving these formidable tasks can thwart, or permanently impede student teaching progress. They should be given top priority in the initial days.

The pupils will also begin a period of adjustment to the new classroom personality. What is he like? What changes will there be? Will he be strict or easy? Above all, they will observe the supervising teacher's reaction to the student teacher. Some pupils will vie for the attention of this new individual. Consequently, the supervising teacher may note that a few pupils are acting differently. As a matter of fact, a new mood may permeate the entire classroom.

New and unique demands are made upon the supervising teacher at this time. The most apparent initial change may be the additional work load that must be assumed. The following details and activities will have to be considered during the first few days:

Conferring with the student teacher
Planning constructive activity for the student teacher
Introducing the student teacher to various members of the faculty and staff
Conferring with the college supervisor when he visits
Acquainting the student teacher with procedures involved in preparation of materials
Beginning to determine a teaching schedule for the student teacher
Arranging initial teaching activities and observations
Becoming operationally familiar with the university handbook for student teachers and requirements of the student teaching program

INTRODUCING THE STUDENT TEACHER TO THE CLASS: **Helping Strangers Meet New Friends**

An introduction of a student teacher does more than present a name to a group of pupils or give the student teacher a chance to offer greetings to a sea of faces. It is a process of communicating feelings and ascribing status. This may be the most obvious clue for the pupils in perceiving the teacher's attitude toward this beginner. Certain words in the introduction can reveal what the supervising teacher actually thinks of the student teacher.

The introduction often is the activity which defines the roles of student teacher, supervising teacher, and pupils. Since it may affect relationships during the entire time that he is participating in the school, it should be carefully planned. These considerations are worthy of emphasis in designing an effective introductory statement:

Welcome the student teacher
   Project the feeling of sincerity and delight at having him as part of the class

Use personal expressions to show a feeling of acceptance

Ask pupils to share in the greeting

Recognize the competency of a student teacher

Specify major areas of study

Describe any particular experiences or achievements related to areas of study

Mention interesting skills the student teacher possesses

Create prestige

The term "practice teacher" should be avoided as it has a derogatory implication

A college senior probably commands more admiration from students than does a student teacher. Emphasize his college standing in your introduction

Indicate confidence in the student teacher

Project the feeling that you know he can work successfully in the classroom

Make the introduction open-ended

Give the student teacher an opportunity to speak to the class if he wishes

Give him latitude to express what he wants to say

The student teacher should be introduced to the class in a way which gives him status and conveys the feeling that he is welcome because he can make a real contribution to the learning process. The following model might serve as a guide in preparing an introduction:

"This morning, we welcome Mr. Brian Sims to our class as a student teacher from State University. Mr. Sims is a college senior who has just completed his course work and should have some ideas for us that will help us while he is here. You might be interested to know that at the university he was a class officer and a writer for the university newspaper. Mr. Sims, it is good to have you with us."

Case Study No. 4: THE STUDENT TEACHER USES HIS IN-TRODUCTION TO EXPLAIN HIS RULES

Your student teacher had displayed some signs of being apprehensive, but you were not concerned because you anticipated some initial reservations. He had indicated his fear about being able to control a class and you had suggested that he should be firm in the beginning. You did not realize how literally he would consider this advice until he made his response to your introduction. Without consulting you, he used this initial appearance to spell out several rules and regulations which he would expect the students to obey. Many are in violation of your procedures, and some simply would not be effective.

What would you do?
1. Make no effort to do anything and assume that he will learn from future experiences
2. Talk with him after class and suggest a revised set of comments for the next contact with the students
3. Attempt to change the introductory statements by injecting some interpretive remarks as you follow up on his comments
4. Correct him during the introduction
5. Affirm to the class that Mr. —————————— is in charge when he is teaching and that he will have complete authority in the classroom
6. _____

Consider:

a. The value of discussion of the student teacher's introductory statement
b. The basic needs of the pupils
c. Methods of arresting a student teacher's insecurity
d. An early conference relating to the topic of delegated authority
e. _____

Case Study No. 5: THE STUDENT TEACHER PROJECTS UNCERTAINTY IN GREETING THE CLASS

The new student teacher was obviously quite reserved. She had answered questions quickly and hesitated to look directly at you when talking. She appeared reluctant to respond to an introduction on the first day, but you felt that it was necessary that she greet the pupils. After you introduce her, she mumbles a few words and sits down quickly. The students appear a bit surprised and look at each other dubiously. Then they look at you. What do you do?

1. Continue as if the response were completely natural
2. Attempt to involve the student teacher in conversation with you and with the class
3. Mention a specific topic you are confident she is familiar with and ask her to comment further
4. Fabricate a reason for her making a hasty response
5. Arrange to be alone with the class soon and explain that she is a learner, too, and determine how you and the class can work together to help her
6. _____

Consider:

a. Techniques of making first encounters as pleasant as possible
b. The effect of each of the above alternatives on pupils and student teacher
c. Planning a successful response

d. Introductory comments which can put a student teacher at ease

e. _____

Case Study No. 6: THE STUDENT TEACHER WHO IS TOO EAGER

Your student teacher possessed supreme confidence in himself. After your introduction he makes an eloquent response:

"Class, it's so pleasant to be with you. I hope you are as enthused as I am. I know that we are going to enjoy working together. I am going to change some old ways of doing things, and we are going to get down to studying some ideas that are really wild."

What is your response?

1. Make no comment about the introduction
2. Endorse the student teacher's enthusiasm
3. Attempt to de-emphasize his comments in your subsequent remarks to the class
4. Give the class an opportunity to interact with him
5. _____

Consider:

a. The type of response the class will probably make
b. Methods of challenging the enthusiastic student so that his actions can be constructive
c. The reason why the student teacher chose those comments for his introduction
d. _____

INTRODUCING THE STUDENT TEACHER TO THE FACULTY: **Meeting the Charter Members of the Club**

A student teacher's contact with other professionals is necessary for a thorough comprehension of a teacher's role. His previous contacts with teachers have been as a student; now he will meet them as a teacher. He may be surprised to learn that they are friendly, sincere and possess a sense of humor. There may be times, however, when he may be disillusioned by the type of conversation he hears from these teachers as they congregate during the school day. He will also gather much information and be exposed to many ideas about teaching through association with these colleagues.

A student teacher's confidence builds as he observes that he has been accepted by the faculty. Teachers' encouragement and support can mean much to a beginner. Other teachers are valuable resource personnel in providing instructional ideas for student teachers. The individual faculty members, often without realizing it, make substantial impressions on the student teachers and affect their outlook toward the teaching profession. Some faculty members may have a special interest in the student teacher. This is particularly likely among those who were graduated from the same school and those who teach the same grade level or subject area. A student teacher can often contribute recent knowledge and ideas which are of interest to the instructional staff.

Introduction to the faculty is not an incidental process. It should be made in a manner that will provide recognition and acceptance of the student teacher. The following procedures may be of value in considering a desirable method of acquainting the student teacher with members of the faculty:

Before the student teacher arrives, indicate that the university is sending a student teacher who will be working with you
> The official school announcement or school newspaper can list the names of future student teachers and their arrival dates
> The impending arrival of a student teacher can be mentioned in casual conversation with teachers

Introduce the student teacher to the faculty
> Faculty meetings
> Informal get-togethers in which student teachers can meet the staff

Make comments that will help a student teacher know and remember a teacher
> Indicate a faculty member's responsibilities when they meet and make a few comments that will serve as cues in recalling that person

See that he meets early the teachers with whom he will be working
Arrange for him to spend time with other teachers without your presence
See that the student teacher knows where the faculty congregates informally and help him feel welcome there

Case Study No. 7: COMMENTS FROM THE TEACHERS' LOUNGE UPSET THE STUDENT TEACHER

The teachers' lounge is generally a good place for student teachers to get to know the faculty. After you make a few introductions, you suggest that the student teacher spend some time there becoming acquainted with the teachers. Her reactions prove to be more negative than positive. When you inquire, she informs you that she is "disgusted" with their unprofessional attitudes. She then proceeds to describe the negative talk about students that she hears and says that she is appalled at the constant criticism of administrative laxness and student ineptness. She cannot understand their cynicism about teaching in general. She was really shocked when one teacher told her that if she were wise she would not go into teaching. How do you respond?

1. Suggest that she cease visiting the lounge
2. Explain that these are the minutes when teachers relax and that their comments should not always be literally interpreted
3. Explain that not all teachers follow a strict code of ethics
4. Talk to the teachers involved when you have the opportunity and inform them of their effect upon the student teacher's attitudes
5. _____

Consider:

  a. Techniques to prepare a student to accept faculty members informally
  b. The extent to which contacts with other teachers should be guided
  c. The idealism of a teaching candidate
  d. _____

INTRODUCING THE STUDENT TEACHER TO TEACHING: **Gingerly into the Stream**

Apprehension is a way of life for students in their initial efforts to teach a class. One student teacher commented to the author that he spilled both his coffee and his juice at breakfast the morning he was to begin student teaching. This anxiety is intensified as the student teacher sits observing his supervising teacher who seems to execute a lesson so effortlessly. Tension may mount as he realizes that he is to fill that individual's position in a few days.

Initial fear is not relieved by the prolonged periods of observation which are all too common in the initial days of student teaching. The reserve on the bench, for instance, may be more excited than the player who is in the midst of the action. Once the reserve enters the game, he may be less nervous and more in command of his feelings. A student teacher's anxiety, like that of the reserve player, will probably remain or increase until he has had some opportunity to experience the teacher's role. Performance in the classroom is the most efficient method of reducing consternation.

In addition to the strain of waiting, the student teacher quickly becomes bored when he has nothing to do. He has been busy and active at college and he is prepared for the same type of activity in student teaching. If he is subjected to nothing but observation of a supervising teacher for days (even hours), he can begin to lose interest.

Introduction into teaching should be a gradual process in which the student teacher immediately begins assuming a few simple activities. As he succeeds in these roles, he can move to more complicated procedures, and finally into a responsible teaching role. He takes several small steps instead of one major one in beginning to work with a class.

The Initial Days

The first day of student teaching is not too early to get the student teacher involved in classroom participation. The student teacher should be given responsibilities which will make a contribution to the class. He should not be made an "errand boy" in actuality or by application. There are many worthwhile teaching activities he can perform without intensive preparation or orientation. Possible early activities include:

Carrying out brief teaching activities
  Making a comment about the lesson content from his perspective
  Providing an illustration for a topic being covered
  Introducing a concept or idea
Distributing and collecting papers
Checking attendance
Supervising study periods
Administering tests and quizzes
Assisting with laboratory or project work
Working with individuals or small groups
Operating equipment
Assisting the teacher with demonstrations
Explaining a specific procedure or technique

The student teacher will find it advantageous to be seated in front of the room, preferably at his own desk or table, from the very first day he is with the class. Sitting in front of the class presents a completely different view of teaching from observation at the rear of the room. This station in the classroom aids the student teacher in making significant observations and contributions since increased awareness of the total teaching process is possible. Some of the more obvious advantages of the student teacher's sitting in front of the room are:

Pupils are more apt to perceive him as a teacher
  An observer in the rear of the room is an "outsider"
He can learn the names of pupils more quickly
He can better perceive the dynamics of the class
The supervising teacher will more likely utilize him as an assistant if he is readily accessible

The student teacher will be formulating impressions about the nature of the class during these first few days. He will be familiarizing himself with the routine procedures and with the techniques of the cooperating teacher. He will need to start devising the processes he will use in adapting to the class style. Explanations of details and procedures are welcomed at this point. Student teachers respond favorably to the supervisor's taking time to explain why he did something or to analyze the results of a particular move in class.

An early task is to determine a suitable teaching schedule. It will first be helpful for the student teacher to know what has been taught prior to his coming, what is to be taught while he is there, and what will be covered after he has completed his experience. This should be combined with available resources so that he can become familiar with the content and begin to start thinking about what and how he will teach. Obviously some early conferences on this topic are required.

Worksheet No. 2: A CHECKLIST FOR THE FIRST FEW DAYS OF STUDENT TEACHING

During the initial period of student teaching, the supervising teacher should have:

1. been aware of the special needs of the student teacher as he adjusts to a different environment
2. introduced the student teacher to his class in such a way that gives him status
3. shown an attitude that indicates that he welcomes the student teacher as a partner in his classroom
4. made a conscious effort to introduce the student teacher to other faculty members and school personnel
5. familiarized the student teacher with the routine and management techniques in his classroom
6. acquainted the student teacher with work currently under way in the class
7. involved the student teacher in classroom participation
8. provided the student teacher with a textbook and a place to work
9. provided the student teacher with a copy of class schedules and a school handbook
10. oriented the student teacher to the school building
11. discussed pertinent school policies and regulations with the student teacher
12. assisted the student teacher in learning the names of pupils
13. included the student teacher in discussions and planning with pupils
14. reached an agreement concerning the responsibility and authority each will have
15. planned for the student teacher's gradual assumption of teaching responsibilities
16. assisted the student teacher in becoming familiar with different available instructional materials
17. oriented the student teacher to the community and assisted him, if neded, in locating living accommodations
18. assisted the student teacher in acquiring background information on the pupils with whom he will be working

Case Study No. 8: TOO ANXIOUS TO BEGIN TEACHING

Cindy is a most enthusiastic beginning student teacher. She says that she is really excited about student teaching and wants to get started immediately. She asks if she can teach her entire teaching schedule on the second day so that she will "know what it's like." You believe that no beginner can successfully assume that much responsibility with only two days of contact with the school. However, she is persistent, and you do not want to crush her enthusiasm, so you are in a real dilemma concerning this request.

What action do you take?

1. Let her take as much responsibility as she wishes and then wait to see if any problems result
2. Counter with the proposal that she begin with smaller amounts of responsibility and then assume additional tasks as she seems capable of handling them
3. Indicate that you have a policy that the student teacher should observe a number of days before assuming responsibility for a class
4. _____

Consider:

a. Evidence of student teacher's potential
b. Techniques of giving responsibility while not delegating an overpowering load
c. The consequences of waiting too long
d. The implications of early failure
e. _____

Case Study No. 9: REACTING TO THE INITIAL EXTENDED PERIOD OF TEACHING

Marge presented her first full lesson to four different sections during her first day of extensive responsibility. She was well prepared and confident. As her supervisor you observe that she seemed to be too concerned about what she was saying and was not aware of whether the students were responding or comprehending. During the last class you sense that she seemed to be somewhat bored by saying the same thing over and over. Since this was her first extended period of teaching, you wonder what kinds of suggestions to offer.

1. Suggestions which tend to be encouraging only
2. Minor suggestions, such as facial expression, asking pupils to speak more loudly, and mannerisms
3. Penetrating suggestions in regard to her lack of attention to pupils and her technique of communication
4. Ask her to analyze herself and support her or offer incidental comments only
5. _____

Consider:

a. The initial effect of a heavy schedule
b. The merits of self-analysis versus teacher analysis
c. The extent to which a number of suggestions can effectively be comprehended
d. The readiness of the student teacher for evaluation
e.

Assuming Responsibility

Student teachers should begin to assume teaching responsibility immediately. Cooperative teaching is one of the key methods whereby a student can assume responsibility without being subjected to consequences should failure result. This arrangement allows both the supervisor and student teacher to share in the responsibility of guiding the learning of pupils. The student teacher should perceive and the pupils should observe that the supervising teacher and student teacher are co-workers. Several types of joint activities can be selected which will achieve such a goal. Many situations are possible that will identify the student teacher and the supervising teacher as co-workers, and several will require little advance organization or planning. The key to success in organizing cooperative teaching is the awareness of its possibility. The following have been practiced by successful supervising teachers:

Planning cooperatively
   Teacher solicits ideas from the student teacher
   Plans are jointly developed
   Each reviews the plans of the other and offers suggestions
   Resources are shared
Teaching as a team
   Supervising teacher works with part of the class and the student
      teacher works with another section
   Joint instruction (presentation by both)
   One teaching and the other demonstrating or assisting
Sharing teaching responsibilities
   Records and reports
   Lunch room supervision
   Directing homeroom activity
*Assigning the student teacher tasks that illustrate the supervising
   teacher's confidence in him*
   Working with pupils who need professional assistance (knowledge,
      creative tasks, learning problems)
   Performing tasks that demand professional competence (operating
      equipment, directing a choir, coaching the team, setting up
      a demonstration)
   Presenting a new idea or concept

Attending faculty meetings and professional meetings
Asking the student teacher to meet the same requirements made of teachers

Obligations demanded of the student teacher should be "real" responsibilities. If he is only asked to perform menial tasks, he will either resent being made a "flunky," become bored with teaching, or assume that he is inadequate. In addition, the student teacher should have the opportunity to assume greater responsibilities as soon as he is able. His proportion of leadership should increase gradually until he has acquired his designated maximum teaching load.

A quick survey of the student teacher's activities can give an appraisal of his progress in his initial adjustment to this new life. If he has assumed normal responsibility, by the end of the second week he should:

Be independent in his movement in the school
    Know the location of key facilities
    Be able to secure most needed materials
Know the names of his students
Have some professional knowledge about his students
Be able to make plans independently of the supervising teacher's direct instruction
Have taken some responsibility for teaching an entire class
Have met a number of other teachers and feel comfortable with them
Have observed teachers in other areas as well as in his major teaching field
Have enough confidence in himself so that he does not become a "shadow" of the supervising teacher

It is not uncommon for a student teacher to be extremely tired at the end of the day. Having been accustomed to a more passive role in the classroom, many student teachers become exhausted in executing their duties. The student teacher should not be overprotected, though, since he needs to discover that fatigue is often a natural part of a teacher's life.

Worksheet No. 3: SUGGESTED EXPERIENCES FOR A TOTAL STUDENT TEACHING PROGRAM

Listed below are a number of experiences which have been considered beneficial for student teachers. Although every situation cannot provide participation in all, this list can serve as a guide in structuring a comprehensive student teaching environment. Many of these activities can be initiated or should be completed during the first few days.

1. The student teacher prepares a seating chart and learns the names of the pupils
2. Studies cumulative records to gain knowledge about pupils

3. Makes a case study of a pupil
4. Discusses his pupils' records with guidance personnel
5. Discusses pupil behavior and progress with the supervising teacher
6. Works with individual pupils and small groups
7. Participates with the supervising teacher in parent conferences
8. Attends and participates in meetings, such as the PTA, where he meets the pupils' parents
9. Attends community activities and social functions
10. Shares in the routine teacher tasks, such as selling milk and collecting fees
11. Takes roll and records attendance
12. Regulates temperature, lighting and other physical aspects of the room
13. Applies techniques of opening and dismissing classes in a systematic and effective manner
14. Helps with problems of discipline and classroom management
15. Assists with extraclass activities such as working at athletic contests, chaperoning social activities, and helping with various clubs
16. Helps supervise playground, cafeteria, corridors, and study hall
17. Participates in pupil groups, such as home rooms and clubs
18. Supervises classroom study
19. Manages a study hall
20. Observes various teachers throughout the school
21. Learns of the work of the special staff, such as the school nurse and speech therapist
22. Develops and uses acceptable writing skills on the chalkboard and overhead projector
23. Prepares a bulletin board or other display
24. Uses different types of technological media
25. Locates and uses supplemental reference materials
26. Learns to use the duplicator
27. Prepares, administers, and scores a classroom test
28. Prepares and uses various teaching aids, compiles a bibliography, and builds a file of supplementary materials
29. Evaluates homework and other assignments
30. Keeps a grade book and builds a file of work completed by pupils
31. Assists with reporting pupil progress
32. Attends faculty and other professional meetings
33. Studies a code of ethics
34. Talks informally with different faculty members concerning the teaching profession
35. Confers with the building principal and other members of the administrative staff
36. Familiarizes himself with professional journals, both in general education and specific fields
37. Observes himself teach by use of the video-tape-recorder
38. Listens to himself teach on an audio recorder
39. Examines several textbooks in his subject field or for a particular grade level

40. Directs some activities without the presence of the supervising teacher
41. Prepares unit and daily plans

Case Study No. 10: ASSISTING THE STUDENT TEACHER WHO AVOIDS ASSUMING RESPONSIBILITY

You have a plan which is designed to give your student teacher gradual induction into complete responsibility. You become concerned, though, when you discover that he resists your suggestions for assuming any type of independent action. He indicates that he would prefer to start with some other activity or would like to wait a little longer. After a few days of excuses, you decide that you must initiate some procedure to get him involved. What do you do?

1. Ask him to suggest activities instead of assigning specific responsibilities
2. Permit him to wait for a period of time as he requests
3. Insist that he needs to assume some responsibilities in order to overcome his hesitation
4. Contact the college supervisor
5. _____

Consider:

a. The causes that seem to be related to the student teacher's reluctance
b. Situations which can be less threatening for the student teacher
c. _____

Ten school days have passed. Brian Sims turns to his required student teaching journal and begins a summary of his first days as a student teacher.

"I feel a little tired right now. I do not think that I have worked so hard or been under as much mental strain in my life. This has been a most hectic period, but it has been most beneficial.

"My supervising teacher, Miss Bennett, is thoughtful and helpful. She has let me help grade papers and kept me informed about all that was happening in the class. After each class she will answer my questions and we have talked about everything concerning teaching that crossed our minds.

"When I was introduced to the class, I spent the first few minutes telling the students about myself. In a few days I had assumed responsibility for teaching one group. I was surprised at myself the first day I taught. I was uneasy, but not like I thought I would be. As a matter of fact, I do not think I appeared to be nervous to the students. Miss Bennett liked my introduction. She described it as formal but friendly. She seems to have confidence in me, and this gives me more assurance.

"I find that I am busy most of the time. When I am not teaching I am usually talking with my supervisor or planning. I take work home most every evening. I have been to a faculty meeting, PTA meeting, and two ball games. No time to get bored."

Remember:

The student teacher must be approached with trust and confidence

Emphasis should be placed on the "we" process--a team working together in the interests of children

Early activities should be planned so that the student teacher does not feel that he is being exploited or neglected

The most effective way of reducing student-teacher anxiety is to give him teaching experience

Boredom sets in rapidly when the student teacher has nothing to do during the first few days of student teaching

Solving small problems early may prevent more complex problems at a later time.

The student teacher is a beginner

The student teacher should be allowed to assume teaching responsibilities gradually

USEFUL REFERENCES

ALTENHEIN, MARGARET RECKLING, "Is Your Teacher Education Classroom a Practical Workshop?" *Peabody Journal of Education* 42:300-303, March, 1965

ASSOCIATION FOR STUDENT TEACHING, *Guiding Student Teaching Experiences,* The Association for Student Teaching Bulletin No. 1, 1969, pp. 6-8, 9-11
> Helping the faculty become acquainted with the student teacher
> The supervising teacher and student teacher get started
> First-day activities for the student teacher
> Responsibilities which can be assumed during the first week
> Determining how rapidly a student teacher can assume responsibility

BATCHELDER, HOWARD T., McGLASSON, MAURICE, AND SCHORLING, RALEIGH, *Student Teaching in Secondary Schools,* McGraw-Hill, New York Chapter Two, 1964
> Moving ahead in student teaching

BROWN, THOMAS J., *Guiding a Student Teacher,* Harper and Brothers, New York, 1960, pp. 10-19
> Introducing a student teacher to teaching

CURTIS, DWIGHT K., AND ANDREWS, L. O., *Guiding Your Student Teacher,* Prentice-Hall, New York, Chaps. 4, 5, 1954
> Helping the student teacher get started
> The student teacher's readiness to teach

MICHIGAN STATE UNIVERSITY, *Handbook for Supervising Teachers,* Chapter 3, Michigan State University, 1968
> Setting the stage and beginning steps

NELSON, LESLIE, AND MacDONALD, BLANCHE, *Guide to Student Teaching,* Chap. 2, William C. Brown Co., 1958
> Orientation to student teaching

SHARPE, DONALD M., *A Brief Guide to Secondary Student Teaching,* Indiana State University, Terre Haute, Indiana, 1970, pp. 11-12
> Introducing a student teacher to the class

STRATEMEYER, FLORENCE B. AND LINDSEY, MARGARET, *Working with Student Teachers,* Teachers College Press, Columbia University, Chap. 7, 1958
> Initial days of student teaching

Chapter Three

ESTABLISHING EFFECTIVE PERSONAL RELATIONSHIPS

Brian and Miss Bennett entered the teachers' lounge and nearly ran into Gordon Rogers, a student teacher from Western who was completing his third week at Central City.

"I've had it," he fumed, as he made a quick exit. "That woman is impossible."

Entering the room, they found an annoyed and exasperated Sally Hawkins, Gordon's supervising teacher, sitting alone at a table. Miss Bennett made a feeble attempt to ease the tension, "I can relax a bit now and then since Brian is here. He is assuming more responsibility and I am looking forward to becoming an observer for a few weeks."

"I wish my student teacher were leaving today," muttered Miss Hawkins. "I am thinking about calling Western and telling them that I can no longer put up with this impudent snob."

"What's the problem, Sally?" inquired Miss Bennett. The response was more than she had anticipated.

"In the first place, he told me that he could be teaching effectively if I had taught the class better before he came. Imagine! This happened when I informed him that the pupils were not understanding his terminology. His plans consist of a few topic outlines, and he dashes them off after he gets to school in the morning. He hangs around with Mr. Reed most of his leisure time--and he seems to find plenty of it." (Mr. Reed is generally considered to be a rather ineffective young teacher.) "He just won't listen to me at all. I tell him what to do and how to do it and all he does is argue with me. If I had wanted my teaching criticized, I would have called in the principal or supervisor. This young upstart is not the expert he thinks he is."

Miss Bennett and Brian exchanged glances but said nothing.

Miss Hawkins continued, "Furthermore, he has been making some immature comments which could have double meanings to the students. And two teachers have asked me not to let him observe them any more because he went to sleep in class."

Miss Bennett interrupted with, "Have you discussed the problems with him or with his college supervisor?"

Miss Hawkins shook her head. "All our conferences end up in arguments. Just now I asked him to explain how two activities were related and he said, 'I don't need a cross-examination. I'm not stupid,' and stormed out. Mr. Williams said that I should call Western and tell them to assign him to another school since he is not cooperating here. I thought I would wait until his supervisor visited again. What would you do?"

"I really don't know," responded Miss Bennett. "Fortunately Brian and I have been able to communicate very well."

Miss Hawkins looked at her, wondering if she were implying that some of her supervisory techniques might have been inappropriate. . .

EFFECTIVE PERSONAL RELATIONSHIPS WITH THE STUDENT TEACHER: **More Than a Friendly "Hello"**

The student teaching experience is a period of adjustment for both student teacher and supervising teacher. The student teacher is becoming familiar with a new environment and is testing his skill in an activity which he has previously not experienced. He is no longer a student but not yet a teacher, and this role confusion can lead to a great deal of uncertainty on his part. He realizes that the classes he teaches are not his and that all his actions ultimately need to have the expressed or implied consent of the supervising teacher. He may find that his personality is very much unlike that of his supervisor, and he may feel more comfortable with younger teachers or even with some pupils.

The supervising teacher may feel pressured by many of the same conditions. The experience of having a student teacher in the room causes some teachers to feel so uncomfortable that sharing a class is a real task. Other cooperating teachers have commented that they are uneasy when the student teacher "shadows" them all the time.

Although the conditions for tension exist, this very association also has the exciting potential for wholesome and enriching contacts between an experienced educator and a teaching candidate. Differences in personality and style can add some zest to a class provided that not all the energy is put into emphasizing the dissimilarities. The supervising teacher, being the more experienced, will normally be the first to recognize the dynamics of a situation and can take the initiative in establishing a constructive emotional climate.

Creating Good Relationships

A good relationship between the student teacher and the supervising teacher is fundamental to a good student teaching environment. It begins with mutual acceptance and understanding and develops as the following conditions become reality:

The student teacher understands that he is not to be a "robot" copying the techniques of the supervising teacher and duplicating his every move

The student teacher works in an environment where he feels neither pushed nor overprotected

The student teacher is accepted as a professional equal

The student teacher is included in more than the immediate environment of the classroom

He may be invited to the supervising teacher's home

He can be included in informal get-togethers with teachers

He might be involved in conversation about topics other than the classes taught or specific concerns relating to his teaching

The student teacher's ideas are encouraged, accepted, and implemented whenever possible

A supervising teacher should show himself to be a human being who has a genuine interest in others. Rarely has a student teacher had a chance to meet a teacher on an equal basis; his view of teachers has been from the perspective of a pupil. They should share their mutual and unique interests, and each should listen to the other, not with condescension, but with genuine interest. Such interchange will free the student teacher to be himself, to be more humanly interesting.

Offering Suggestions in a Constructive Climate

Every supervising teacher will eventually be faced with the necessity of having to offer criticism or give advice to the student teacher. Many teachers wonder whether a direct approach can lead to a deterioration of relationships so that effective communication becomes more difficult. The attitude of the student teacher is often the clue to the selection of a desirable procedure. Too much "preaching" or "dictating" can lead to defensive reactions, but a lack of any conversation or suggestions may cause the student teacher to be suspicious or depressed. There is no single formula for creating ideal personal relationships with a student teacher since personalities of real people are involved.

The following alternatives may be helpful in producing an environment which is more tension-free:

Criticism given in the presence of others should be avoided
Criticism should be an attempt to build a person up instead of discouraging him from trying
The climate should be one of "working together on a problem" instead of "criticizing an individual's efforts"
Emotion-producing words or actions should be avoided, except in the possible utilization of humor

The supervising teacher must avoid being hypercritical. Constant censure is likely to cause a student teacher to become resistant or to retreat from productive analysis, thus thwarting progress toward the goal of self-evaluation. Since a student teacher almost never commits an error that is irreparable, extreme and continuous criticism seem inconsistent with the aim of being evaluative in a constructive context.

Personality Conflicts

It is extremely difficult to be completely objective when personality conflicts exist because the problem rests with the feelings of the personnel who are involved. An atmosphere can develop where flexibility becomes secondary and rigidity predominates. It is common knowledge that some people find certain types of personalities abrasive and they have difficulty establishing effective communication with them. It can become very complicated when two such individuals are assigned to work together as student teacher and supervisor. There are certain moves which a supervising teacher can initiate which can potentially improve such a situation or at least make it more acceptable:

Proclaim the difference and accept it
　A little tension can be constructive provided it is acknowledged and
　　accepted by both parties.
*Attempt to circumvent or embellish differences instead of placing direct
　energy into the conflict*
*Discover methods of communication which will place less emphasis on
　personality conflict*
　Written communication
　Non-directive techniques
*Plan autonomous activities so that both have independent responsi-
　bility but the supervising teacher can still observe performance*
　Supervisor works with half the class; student teacher works with the
　　other half
*Arrange for the student teacher to have some time with other teachers
　with whom he can feel more comfortable*

Case Study No. 11: THE STUDENT TEACHER CRITICIZES HER SUPERVISING TEACHER

　　Sandy was not happy as a student teacher because she felt that her supervising teacher was too critical of her. She described the situation to her college supervisor and said that she was not given enough freedom to determine her own style. She said that the teacher criticized her for everything from poor planning to improper dress. She remarked that her supervising teacher even insisted that she eat lunch with her when she would prefer to meet with some of the other teachers whom she had met.

　　The college supervisor feels that he should interpret those feelings to you, her supervisor, and informs you during a private conference. You are surprised at this because you felt that she had been depending on you for security. Furthermore it was she who had been initiating the idea that the two of you have lunch together every day.

　　Confronted with this difference, what do you do?

1. Explain your position to the college supervisor
2. Encourage her to be more independent by offering fewer suggestions regarding her professional and personal decisions
3. Ask the college supervisor to place her with another teacher
4. Discuss the differences of opinion with her
5. Ignore the comments, assuming that the perceptions of the college supervisor may have been erroneous
6. ―――――――――――――――――――――――――――

Consider:

a. Reasons for the conflicting impressions
b. Analysis of procedures used in supervision and their possible implications
c. Learning more about the student teacher
d. ——————————————————————————

Case Study No. 12: THE STUDENT TEACHER IDENTIFIES CLOSELY WITH ANOTHER TEACHER

Your student teacher appeared a little uncomfortable with you from the beginning, and he seemed to be ill-at-ease in his contacts with several other teachers. He did develop a close relationship with one of the young teachers in your area in the building, however. They seem to have a lot in common and you observe that your student teacher appears to be avoiding you in order to be with the other teacher. There is evidence also that he is talking over his problems with this teacher.

Since you feel that a closer communication needs to be developed between you and the student teacher, what course of action do you pursue?

1. Inform the student teacher that the two of you need to spend more time together in conference
2. Take steps to arrange for specific times when the two of you are together both formally and informally
3. Ignore the situation
4. Talk to the other teacher and explain the problem which seems to be developing
5. ——————————————————————————

Consider:

a. The reasons for a student teacher gravitating to another teacher
b. The possible ramifications of this closeness with a younger teacher
c. The implications of intervention in a personal relationship
d. ——————————————————————————

Case Study No. 13: THE STUDENT TEACHER DISPLAYS A NEGATIVE REACTION TO ATTEMPTS AT COMMUNICATION

In spite of your best attempts, your student teacher has been difficult to reach. Your efforts at constructive analysis have caused her to project blame to pupils or to state that she is not supposed to be proficient in those areas. References to subject matter have caused her to say that she would not get any background in that until she completes some additional course work on campus next semester. Her responses are abrupt and tend to close conferences rather than encourage dialogue. One day you learn on good authority that she feels that you are picking on her. This news causes you to take some action.

What do you decide to do?

1. Directly confront her about her negative reactions
2. Ask her to explain why she feels she is being harassed and attempt to discover her problems
3. Examine her records thoroughly for cues to her behavior
4. Consult the college supervisor concerning her behavior
5. Avoid any evaluative comments for a period of time
6. _____

   Consider:

   a. The possibility that the basic cause originates from something yet unknown
   b. Whether any of her student teaching experiences have contributed to a building of security
   c. Alternative types of communication
   d. _____

EFFECTIVE PERSONAL ADJUSTMENT: **Looking at Teaching Through Rose-Colored Glasses**

Student teaching involves the entire being of a person. A student teacher's feelings and beliefs will determine his basic approach to teaching and permeate every activity related to the professional experience. It is perfectly reasonable for the dimension of feeling to be interjected into the student teaching act. The student teacher should not attempt to merely be a walking textbook. He must endeavor to inspire as well as instruct. If he fails to do the one, he will probably fail in the other. The quality of beliefs and feelings of the student teacher determines the procedures and content of a lesson just as much as a chapter in a textbook or prior learning at the university.

Overt expressions of feelings are more changeable than underlying beliefs. The supervising teacher may frequently observe changes in feelings which have resulted from some personal situation or from a recent experience. The supervising teacher is not expected to be a professional analyst, but he may be in a position to influence feelings and modify behavior. Awareness of the student teacher as a person and an understanding of the nature of his feelings can lead to procedures which can cause the student teacher to react to teaching in a more human way.

A yearbook of the Association for Student Teaching reported a study of the problems which "bug" student teachers most. Ten of the 18 statements reported related directly to personal adjustment:

Being accepted by the cooperating teacher only as a student
Not being accepted as a person
Personal feeling of inadequacy
Accepting criticism from cooperating teacher
The unfavorable attitude of the faculty toward them

The feeling of not belonging
Not being encouraged to participate in appropriate teachers' commit-
  tees
The feeling of not belonging because they were not invited to attend
  faculty and social events
Being omitted from the distribution list of school announcements
Having to ask permission to use the telephone[1]

This report lends support to the contention that the profession in general and supervising teachers in particular may be overlooking the deep feelings and anxieties of the student teachers. These statements illustrate the student teachers' concern for relationships with other people and for maintaining their own sense of worth.

These immediate expressions may be symptoms of the predominant feelings of a student teacher. In order to cope with specific difficulties, a supervising teacher may need to identify and understand some of the broader personal concerns of a student teacher. The following seem to categorize the personal problems expressed most frequently by student teachers:

Economic problems
Family conflicts
Problems related to romance
Feelings of inferiority
Feelings of social inadequacy
Concerns about contemporary affairs
Problems related to potential teaching difficulties
Anxiety about future employment or military status
Fears
    of not being able to control a class
    of not being able to answer students' questions
    of running out of material and having time left in a period
    of making mistakes
    of being unable to perform as well as the supervising teacher

There is no formula which will always be successful, but once the supervising teacher has identified his student teacher's problems, a logical plan can possibly be developed which may help adjust to his uneasiness. Accomplishments will be apparent in problem solving to the degree that the supervising teacher and student teacher are willing to attempt to work for an effective solution. There are several moves which the supervising teacher can make which can enhance the possibility of progress or which may correct some of the worries with a minimum of difficulty:

1 Association for Student Teaching. **Mental Health and Teacher Education,** Association for Student Teaching. 46th Yearbook, 1967. p. 5.

Discuss the problem with the student teacher in an objective manner
  Discover what is bothering him
  Analyze the cause
  Discuss possible alternatives in attempting to reach a solution or
    course of action
Treat the student teacher as a peer and not as an inferior
Recognize and demonstrate confidence in the student teacher
Provide situations in which the student teacher can experience success
Encourage him whenever possible
Be available for conversation and discussion
  Encourage the student teacher to talk over the problems he feels
Be a good listener
Show a sincere interest in the problem
Know the facts before action is taken
See that the student teacher feels accepted and needed
Capitalize on special skills or interests
Specify plans of action which will possibly alleviate the difficulty
Try to put problems in a proper context
Be flexible

It may appear from the above discussion that the student teacher may have so many problems that they could not be solved by a professional counselor performing full-time service. Actually many of the teaching worries are lessened through normal student teaching experience in a constructive environment since anticipation causes greater anxiety than the reality of the actual situation.

Perhaps the most important concern for the supervising teacher in the area of human relations is to recognize that the student teacher is a human being whose new surroundings are creating new problems and restructuring old ones. These personal matters will be reflected in the day-by-day relations with the supervising teacher and will affect the approach to the pupils and to the concept of teaching in general. The objective is satisfactory adjustment which will bring about a more wholesome outlook on life and teaching.

Case Study No. 14: "MR. BIG"

So many student teachers begin their experience by attempting to impress their associates and pupils. Your student teacher was really overdoing it, though. He used all the college jargon that he knew and made frequent references to his "mod" life on campus. He seized upon opportunities in the teachers' cafeteria to criticize the Establishment and to provide easy answers for complex questions. He pretended to know more than he obviously did in regard to education. Both students and faculty are beginning to complain to you about his behavior.
  What do you do?

1. Have a direct talk with him and tell him that his behavior
   must change

2. Video-tape his class in the hope that he may see some of these factors being manifest in the classroom
3. Ask him to have the students write an appraisal of him
4. Compliment his good performance in the hope that he will cease to feel a need to present such a facade
5. Attempt to keep him away from some of the more critical members of the faculty and student body
6. ─────────────────────────────────────

Consider:

a. Techniques of discussing the actual problem
b. Reasons for his strong feelings and actions
c. Techniques which can be employed which could reduce the impact of some indiscreet actions
d. ─────────────────────────────

Case Study No. 15: THE EXTREMELY TIMID STUDENT TEACHER

Paul was extremely timid. He tried to make himself as inconspicuous as possible at all times. He was alone as much as he could be and when he was with others, he had nothing to say. As a matter of fact, he did not even appear to be listening. His voice projection was low in the classroom and he hardly looked up as he spoke. His performance was similar in conferences with you. Obviously he is presently too shy to become an effective teacher. He will have to change before he can successfully enter the profession.

What do you do in this situation?

1. Suggest that he consider some position other than teaching
2. Attempt to build his confidence by placing him in situations where he can succeed
3. Tell him that he will have to "sink or swim" and force him into challenging situations
4. Attempt to discover the reasons for his timidity and then work on a possible solution
5. Discuss the situation with the pupils and encourage their assistance in helping him overcome his feelings of timidity
6. ─────────────────────────────────────

Consider:

a. Possible situations which will help a shy individual overcome his fears
b. Responsibility to pupils and the school
c. Contacting the university for assistance
d. Professional situations in which a shy person can make a contribution
e. ─────────────────────────────

Case Study No. 16: THE STUDENT TEACHER WHO IS TOO WELL-ADJUSTED

You have worked hard at making Susie's student teaching experience happy and successful. You apparently succeeded too well. She has had no real difficulties and she is convinced that teaching is relatively tension-free and everything about the school is marvelous. She is really anticipating next year and you have reason to believe that she thinks that it will be as simple and exciting as her student teaching. At this point you begin to wonder if you have not overprotected her and begin to question whether you have really been fair to her.

What course of action do you now take?

1. Do nothing, assuming that her conception of the ideal will provide a better frame of reference for any teaching situation
2. Try to arrange for some experiences which will help her realize some of the problems of teaching and some of her own inadequacies
3. Describe the unrealistic aspects of her student teaching experience and explain what she might logically have to face next year
4. Arrange for her to observe some troublesome classes in the school
5. Arrange for her to talk with some beginning teachers
6. _____

   Consider:

   a. The merits of positive versus the merits of negative learning
   b. Types of activities which present a full range of experience so that a complete profile can be revealed
   c. _____

EFFECTIVE PERSONAL RELATIONSHIPS WITH PUPILS: **The View from the Other Side of the Desk**

The student teacher may be only a few days away from the fraternity or sorority house or college residence hall. A student teacher may appear at the school looking like a teacher, but this appearance does not guarantee that he has similarly acquired more adult behavior patterns. Initially, he is merely a college student who is dressed up, painfully aware that some of his pupils are not much younger than he is. High school students may appear larger than he had remembered and more sophisticated than he had assumed. Facing elementary pupils may cause every learned principle of psychology and methodology to be temporarily disbelieved. The pupils call him a teacher, the university personnel regard him as a student, and the supervising teacher may consider him as a teacher one moment and a student the next.

The problem of adjusting to the students frequently presents a real dilemma for the inexperienced student teacher. Motivated by the desire to be accepted but admonished to get respect by being tough, he may find himself vacillating from one position to the other or wavering just enough to betray his true feelings. Perhaps his greatest error is pretending to be someone other than the person he really is.

The intial classroom stance assumed by the student teacher is dictated more by a concern for survival than by a desire to direct an exciting, interesting, or informative class. The student teacher may be tempted to assume a role which he has found to be effective in achieving acceptance in other situations. This is usually a predicament involving peer acceptance in which he is actually attempting to establish a completely different relationship with people than is appropriate in student teaching. The techniques which have worked in college to impress others are often the ones that will cause him to be ridiculed by pupils. The sad result may be that there is a complete breakdown in respect for the student teacher as an adult. His intense desire to be accepted causes him to be rejected.

Occasionally a student teacher will attempt the "hard line" approach in which he sets down rules and suspends all privileges until the pupils have proved that they are willing to do what he says. Theoretically he then relaxes his standards and becomes more tolerant. The problem is that he will probably be too insecure to be either convincing or authoritative, and he may find himself entangled in a web of unrealistic demands and unenforceable rules.

The task of the supervising teacher is to help the student teacher develop a more comprehensive outlook in the area of pupil-teacher relationships in the school environment. The following procedures are worthy of consideration in assisting the student teacher:

Arrange for the student teacher to assume complete responsibility gradually
    Cooperative arrangements should allow pupils to accept the student teacher as they accept the regular teacher
    The student teacher should be able to conduct frequent brief teaching sessions better than one long period
Try to identify any potential extreme forms of behavior in advance and counsel with the student teacher before he makes a commitment
Help him to understand that students want him to be a sincere adult; not one of them nor an aloof tyrant
Help him to recognize that genuine respect from a class is achieved from such factors as enthusiasm, sincere interest in and respect for people, and interesting class sessions

Out-of-class contacts also present occasional difficulties. It is not uncommon for a beginning student teacher to wonder if discipline will deteriorate if he speaks to one of his pupils when they meet elsewhere. Male student teachers in high schools are frequently the targets of affection from teen-age girls and may be tempted to see them socially. An insecure or immature student teacher may gravitate to the company of the pupils, avoiding the more uncomfortable contacts with adult teachers. At times he may innocently become the victim of an amorous member of the opposite sex in such innocent-sounding requests as being asked for extraclass assistance, to be taken home after an evening meeting, or even in the seemingly innocuous act of sitting with a student on a fan bus to a ball game.

The alert supervising teacher will be aware of this possibility and will attempt to provide a satisfactory set of guidelines for the student teacher's informal contacts with pupils. The student teacher may need to become aware of potential problem situations and learn techniques for achieving satisfactory solutions. He can profit from explanation of procedures for greeting and talking with pupils informally. The student teacher who is uncertain about what to say to the individual whom he meets in out-of-class situations may need to recognize as well the subtle ways a member of the opposite sex (both boys and girls) can create situations which make it appear that the student teacher has not acted with discretion. Keep in mind that he will be ever conscious of the supervisor's approach and may make decisions on the basis of that example. Ethical behavior becomes more than an abstract term at this point.

Case Study No. 17: A STUDENT TEACHER IS ADDRESSED BY HER FIRST NAME

Your student teacher has been attempting to establish rapport with the pupils by displaying a genuine friendliness with them. She has been generally successful and the pupils seem to like her and enjoy their contacts with her. All went well until some of the students discovered that her first name was Carol. A few of them have taken the liberty of calling her by her first name in some informal situations. Carol is concerned now because she realizes that pupils do not address teachers by their first names and she fears that this may lead to a deterioration of respect for her. She asks for your advice about what to do. What course of action do you take?

1. Talk with the pupils involved and demand that they accord her the respect due a teacher
2. Suggest that she explain that they can best support her as a friend if they do not ask for the liberty of a first-name approach
3. Tell her to firmly inform them that her name is "Miss Smith"
4. Suggest that she ignore the pupils whenever possible
5. ————————————————————————

Consider:

a. The importance the student teacher may place on such an incident
b. The motives of the pupils
c. The personalities of the pupils involved
d. The best way for a student teacher to regain her feeling of prestige
e. _____

Case Study No. 18: "YOU ARE ONLY A STUDENT TEACHER"

Your student teacher was in the room alone with the class when she made an assignment that a few of the students objected to. She explained that it was required and would be counted as part of the grade. The pupils countered with, "I don't believe that; you are only a student teacher; Miss Haynes is the teacher and she will give grades." Your student teacher again stated the requirements and continued with the class, but was very upset by the challenge.
What do you do?

1. Support her in what she did
2. Talk to the class and define the student teacher's role clearly
3. Indicate that she must prove that she is the teacher by her own actions and that she cannot be too dependent on you.
4. Talk privately with the pupils involved
5. _____

Consider:

a. The responsibilities and status of the student teacher as she perceives them
b. The attitude of the class toward a student teacher
c. Methods of helping the student teacher gain confidence
d. _____

Case Study No. 19: A GIRL IS DISTURBED BY THE CONDUCT OF A FEW BOYS

Sherri is an attractive blonde who is student teaching in your class. One section has a number of boys in it who are obviously attracted to her and who have become aggressive to gain her attention. She interprets this behavior as a challenge to her authority and attempts to discipline them. Unfortunately, she is not successful and the boys are enjoying her frustration. She comes to you in tears after one of them called her "Sweetie".
What do you do?

1. Talk to the class and demand that they cease such behavior

2. Explain your hypothesis concerning their behavior and suggest techniques of overcoming their desire for attention
3. Attend class and discipline any boy who becomes too aggressive
4. Suggest that she return their comments in kind and they will probably cease because of embarrassment
5. Suggest certain measures which she can deploy
6. Remove her from that particular section
7. _____

Consider:

a. The student teacher's perception of the situation
b. The method which will provide the best security for the student teacher
c. Effective methods of interacting with boys in a professional manner
d. _____

Case Study No. 20: THE STUDENT TEACHER INVITES A FEMALE STUDENT TO A SOCIAL FUNCTION

Your student teacher is a personable individual and has been the center of a lot of attention from a clique of girls. Finally, one of them became very friendly with your student teacher and he obviously was enjoying it. They talked frequently during the day and the girl often came by after school. Extracurricular activities sometimes brought them together in the evenings. One day your student teacher tells you that he would like to invite her to be his date at an event he plans to attend in another community. He asks for your opinion. What do you tell him?

1. Indicate that his personal life is no concern of yours
2. Describe the possible professional implications
3. Project the possible deterioration in student rapport if certain pupils learn that he has dated one of their peers
4. Approve a date at non-school locations, but discourage any such behavior at the school
5. _____

Consider:

a. School policies concerning teacher-student relationships
b. Professional ethics
c. Possible implications upon the specific teaching situation
d. _____

Case Study No. 21: CONFLICT BETWEEN THE STUDENT TEACHER AND THE CLASS

The seventh-hour class had never been a favorite of your student teacher. The conflict between them had been developing for several days, and it came to direct confrontation with a test review. A defensive explanation of a questionable test item led to an angry response from several pupils. The student teacher attempted to shout them down, but he failed. You pass by the door and observe that he is in trouble. What course of action do you take?

1. Walk quietly into the classroom, but make no immediate gesture to the class
2. Demand that the class get quiet
3. Take over the class and discuss the problem
4. Walk on by and do nothing until you have a chance to talk with the student teacher
5. _____

   Consider:

   a. Techniques of preventing such confrontations
   b. Whether the student teacher understands how to cope with the dynamics of the class
   c. The effect of intervention on the confidence of the student teacher
   d. _____

Brian and Miss Bennett headed for the lunch room and were stopped for a moment by a student who had a question about a homework assignment. Brian was still aware of the incident they had witnessed a few moments ago between Gordon Rogers and Sally Hawkins.

"Pardon me if I seem impertinent," Brian began, "but I'm glad that I have you as my supervising teacher instead of some others I have seen."

"You are good natured enough to work with almost anyone, Brian," countered Miss Bennett. "But this business of effective personal relationships is frequently overlooked. If either party becomes defensive, I can see where some real problems can develop."

"We have not always agreed on everything, but I've always felt that you respected me. And even when I took exception to some of your ideas, you were tolerant," commented Brian, "and you certainly have made me aware of how important it is to be a human being as well as a teacher. That is one of the most valuable lessons I have learned."

As they turned into the cafeteria, Miss Bennett dismissed the praise by remarking, "One thing that we have always agreed on is the quality of food in the cafeteria. It has a way of creating consensus among people who generally disagree on most things."

They picked up a wet tray and nodded toward the chili in preference to the hot dogs supreme.

Remember:

A good example is better than a thousand words in personal relationships

Student teaching is a tremendous environment for students and teachers to experience growth in personal relationships with both adults and youth

A student teacher cannot make maximum development if he is treated in a condescending manner

The supervising teacher and student teacher must identify with each other in their thoughts, attitudes, and acts if they are to work as a successful team

The student teacher is a peer, though an inexperienced one

Differences in personalities should be utilized as an asset instead of being considered a problem

What is generally considered to be good taste is also good policy in working with a student teacher

Honesty, thoughtfulness, and tact affirm and help establish and maintain good personal relationships

Student teaching is generally considered to significantly alter the personality of a student teacher

USEFUL REFERENCES

ASSOCIATION FOR STUDENT TEACHING, *Mental Health and Teacher Education,* Association for Student Teaching Yearbook, 1967, Chapter One
  The classroom teacher, mental health, and learning

ASSOCIATION FOR STUDENT TEACHING, *The Student Teacher and Human Relations,* Association for Student Teaching Bulletin No. 26, 1966
  Principles of human relations
  Situations where principles of human relations are reflected

BROWN, THOMAS J., *Student Teaching in a Secondary School,* Harper and Brothers, 1960, Chapter One
  Emotional problems of student teachers

CARPENTER, E. V., AND GUESS, W., "Student Teachers Are People Too!" *Business Education World* 48:29-30, January, 1963

CROW, LESTER D., AND CROW, ALICE, *The Student Teacher in the Elementary School,* David McKay Co., 1965, Chapters 3, 5
  Relationships with pupils
  Relationships with colleagues

CURTIS, DWIGHT, AND ANDREWS, L. O., *Guiding Your Student Teacher,* Prentice-Hall, 1954, Chapter 11
  Building professional relations

DEVOR, JOHN W., *The Experience of Student Teaching,* Macmillan Co., 1964, Chapter 7
  Interpersonal relations

DRAYER, ADAM, *Problems and Methods in High School Teaching,* D. C. Heath and Company, 1963, Chapter 6
  Problems of adjustment to high school personnel

LOWTHER, MALCOLM A., "Successful and Unsuccessful Experiences of Student Teachers in Secondary Education," *Contemporary Education* 41:272-275, May, 1970.
  Success in student teaching as determined by personal relationships

SORENSON, GARTH, AND HALPERT, RUTH, "Stress in Student Teaching," *California Journal of Educational Research* 19:28-33, January, 1968
  Pattern of psychological discomfort during student teaching

STRATEMEYER, FLORENCE B., AND LINDSEY, MARGARET, *Working with Student Teachers,* Teachers College Press, Columbia University, 1958, Chapters 4, 16
  College students as learners

Guiding the student teacher in the transition from college student to member of the profession

STROUSE, JOHN P., "Human Relations in the Student Teaching Triad", *Supervisors Quarterly* 6:3, Spring, 1971, pp 12-15

YOUNG, JAMES H., "Authoritarianism in Elementary Student Teachers and Their Supervising Teachers", *Journal of Teacher Education* 22:1, Spring, 1971, pp 70-71

Chapter Four

WORKING WITH THE COLLEGE SUPERVISOR

The morning session had just started and Brian was beginning his introduction to a new unit of study. Although this would not be his poorest lesson, he knew that it would not be the best one he had ever taught. Finding the right approach had been difficult, and he was by no means convinced that the activities would move smoothly. He looked up from attendance check just in time to see the door open and he observed that a familiar figure moved to a seat in the back of the room. He looked, forced a smile, and tried to conceal his sudden apprehension. Not his college supervisor today! What will he think of this class? Why couldn't he have come yesterday when the lesson was so well developed?

Miss Bennett whispered a word of greeting to Dr. Phillips and handed him a copy of Brian's plan. She then excused herself from the class, indicating that Brian might be more comfortable if there were only one supervisor in the room. Dr. Phillips indicated that they would confer after the class was over.

A few minutes after the class had ended, Dr. Phillips entered Miss Bennett's room for a conference. They talked informally for a while, and then Dr. Phillips opened his folder to his notes and began to inquire about Brian's progress.

THE COLLEGE SUPERVISOR: **The Man Who "Checks Up"**

The exact role of the college supervisor probably has been in need of clarification ever since a college first designated a staff member to coordinate the program of student teaching. He is constantly greeted by principals, teachers, and student teachers as the man who "checks up" on the student teacher. Many supervisors have experienced the unwritten law of "non-betrayal" of the student teacher in which teachers and pupils alike cooperate to see that a good image of the student teacher is presented while his college supervisor is in the building. This unwritten pact assumes that the college supervisor will penalize the student teacher if any of his difficulties or problems are revealed. The student teacher, as well, may choose to offer no critical remarks about his supervising teacher or of the actual educational environment in the mistaken belief that his condition might become worse. It is even no surprise for the college supervisor to learn that the pupils were more cooperative during his visit than they are in the normal course of events. Even the pupils team up to protect the student teacher from the college supervisor! College supervisors need the cooperation of the school personnel instead of being the objects of deception.

The college supervisor's role is a complex one involving several activities and responsibilities. The supervisor himself usually perceives one of his essential roles to be a liaison person. He interprets the university program to the cooperating school; likewise he explains the cooperating school's program to the appropriate personnel at the university. He is also an intermediary between the supervising teacher and the student teacher.

The college supervisor views one of his most-frequently-performed roles as that of a public relations person. The perceptive supervisor is conscious that he may convey the only image of the university which many people will see. The university may well be judged on the basis of his actions. He must work closely with school administrators in promoting good relations between the school and his institution. He is also a university representative in contacts with other school personnel, and he is often asked to explain such varying details as admission requirements and specific services rendered by various branches of his university.

The role that he would probably most prefer to perform is that of supervisor. His visits to the school are best if they are made when he can assist the student teacher in the improvement of instruction and the development of teaching competencies. His experience and knowledge can be of value to the young student teacher who is fumbling with technique. Supervising teachers need to be aware of the fact that he is familiar with the most recent thinking concerning teaching which would enrich the classroom environment.

The college supervisor should obviously be involved in helping the student teacher with his work. He has been described as a guide, confidant, and trouble shooter. His availability and his knowledge of the teaching process can be of inestimable assistance to the student teacher. If a candidate has a particular problem, the supervisor may be in a position to help him reconcile it, or at least to provide some alternative plans of action.

The typical college supervisor is also a part-time administrator. This role involves the process of interviewing and assigning student teachers and seeing that university and state requirements are being adhered to. On occasion he will need to interpret policy concerning the logical course of action in a particular situation.

The general concepts of role break down into specific functions which are performed. Although the responsibilities will vary from institution to institution, the following are most typical:

Interviews candidates for student teaching and recommends assignments
  Makes judgments about the type of assignment needed by a student
  Communicates with members of the student's academic department and his counselor regarding his potential and his projected assignment
  Searches for schools and teachers who can provide the type of experience needed

Orients student teachers to their assignments
  Explains requirements
    Interprets forms
    Makes suggestions concerning the initial contact with the school
    Gives general suggestions regarding the technique of achieving a
      meaningful experience
    Alerts student teachers to the possibility and necessity of adapting
      to the unique features of the school and community
Acquaints supervising teachers with their responsibilities
    Explains the college student teaching program and requirements
    Shares unique information about the student teacher
    Helps determine the schedule for the student teacher
    Suggests desirable types of activities
Counsels with the student teachers concerning problems of adjustment
Assists student teachers in development of instructional techniques
    Observes student teachers' classes, studies their written work, con-
      fers with them and their supervisors
    Helps in the development of teaching skills
Helps student teachers learn to evaluate themselves
Helps supervising teachers evaluate their student teachers
Leads seminars with student teachers

The college supervisor may have had recent experience as a public
school teacher and supervisor of student teachers and is probably
aware of the latest trends in the field. He normally will possess a broad
knowledge of practices and programs in the schools in his area. A good
supervisor will also be familiar with a wide range of ideas in teaching
methodology and may be a good resource person for the public schools.
He should not be overlooked as a possible consultant on curricular, instructional, and organizational matters in the public schools.

Case Study No. 22: THE STUDENT TEACHER BECOMES EX-
CEPTIONALLY ANXIOUS ABOUT THE COLLEGE SUPER-
VISOR'S VISIT

"I know I should not be so worried, but I just get scared
when I think about his coming. I am convinced that I will freeze
when he walks into the classroom."
    The above statement was made to you by your student
teacher. His teaching progress seems to be satisfactory and
there is no apparent reason for him to have a fear of the college
supervisor, but he is quite anxious about any visits from university personnel. What do you do to attempt to help this situation?

1. Tell him that he will get over his fears by simply teaching
   as he had planned
2. Inform the supervisor in advance of any observation, so
   that he will understand the feeling when he observes

3. Cover for the student teacher when the college supervisor visits and then explain that he is anxious about teaching in his presence
4. Arrange to have some other teachers observe so that the student teacher can become more accustomed to having another person visit his class
5. _____

Consider:

a. Reasons for this concern
b. Ways of supervising which can help the student teacher reduce his anxiety
c. Techniques of communicating with the college supervisor about a problem of this type
d. _____

ASSISTING THE STUDENT TEACHER: **Big Daddy or Big Brother?**

The college supervisor will be aware of the fact that he must assist the student teacher in developing teaching competency. Since each student teacher will reveal a different pattern of needs and abilities, the college supervisor must be able to analyze the situation and determine the type of assistance he should offer. He will then employ his knowledge, skill, and resources to attempt to help the student teacher. In order for him to expend the best effort efficiently, he will need to know the student teacher and be acquainted with the dynamics of the teaching situation. This will necessitate his spending time in the classroom and in conference with the student teacher and the supervising teacher.

The college supervisor encourages the student teacher to go beyond a superificial appraisal of teaching into a more intellectual approach, to think about what he is doing, to see relationships, and to formulate plans of action for subsequent experience. The college supervisor can be the catalyst which causes the student teacher to formulate a broader perspective on teaching through reflection about his current experience.

A common practice among universities is the inclusion of a seminar as part of the professional experience. The seminar, or seminars, provides an opportunity for college supervisors to see their student teachers in a different environment and to deal with the immediate concerns of student teaching. The well-structured seminar can provide a situation where the candidates for teaching may compare notes, ask questions, and formulate conclusions through interaction with their peers. The college supervisor uses the seminar to answer questions and guide the dialogue for meaningful analysis of problems. The seminar also affords an opportunity for the college supervisor to suggest new alternatives for teaching practice.

In spite of his most sincere efforts, the college supervisor frequently has difficulty gaining the complete confidence of the student teacher. The concept of supervision is usually remote to the student teacher and he may interpret all the moves of the college supervisor as threatening or evaluative. He cannot escape the feeling that he is being judged and that he must defend every action. In some cases, opportunities for pre-student-teaching contact have been limited and he may not know the supervisor well enough to have confidence in him. Establishing rapport is an obvious task for the effective college supervisor.

The college supervisor attempts to render assistance to the student teacher in various ways. The typical types of procedures are the ones indicated below:

Gives personal assistance
   Answers questions concerning requirements and details
   Calls attention to alternatives in personal considerations in student teaching
   Counsels when problems exist
Works in the development of teaching skills
   Attempts to help the student teacher develop competency in various teaching situations
   Calls attention to teaching resources and ideas
   Observes and analyzes classes with student teachers
Serves as an intermediary in any disputes or misunderstandings between the student teacher and the supervising teacher
Helps the student teacher evaluate his performance and goals

Case Study No. 23: THE STUDENT TEACHER REJECTS THE SUGGESTIONS OF HIS COLLEGE SUPERVISOR

The college supervisor spent several hours visiting your student teacher's classes and conferring with each of you. His primary concern appeared to be to help the student teacher improve in some of his weaker areas, and his suggestions offered alternatives which could lead to better performance. After he leaves, your student teacher appears to be very disturbed and feels that the college representative has been too critical of him. His final comment was, "How can he make any valid judgments?' He wasn't here long enough to know what this class is like."

Since you recognize some validity in the supervisor's suggestions, what moves do you make?

1. Appear non-committal, hoping that this action will create confidence for a later, more objective analysis of his comments
2. Specifically state that you feel that his suggestions have merit and encourage the student teacher to follow the recommendations which were made

3. Attempt to analyze the suggestions and determine their validity in a context which the student teacher might understand

4. _____

Consider:

a. Techniques of building the confidence of the student teacher
b. Techniques of effective communication
c. The intensity of concern felt by the student teacher
d. _____

Case Study No. 24: THE STUDENT TEACHER TAKES THE COLLEGE SUPERVISOR'S SUGGESTIONS TOO SERIOUSLY

After the college supervisor had left, your student teacher began to worry. His interpretation of the supervisor's suggestions was that his work was unsatisfactory and that he might fail student teaching. You indicate that he was offering suggestions for improvement, but he counters with a statement indicating that the supervisor is probably right in assuming that his teaching is below an acceptable level of performance. What do you do to attempt to counteract this feeling?

1. Ignore it, assuming that he will change his attitude with further reflection
2. Assume that his feelings are correct and discuss how teaching improvement might be achieved in the future
3. Contact the college supervisor and inform him of your student teacher's feelings

4. _____

Consider:

a. Techniques of presenting an accurate interpretation of the visit
b. Methods of changing the student teacher's attitude
c. Procedures which might be used in effecting improvement in the student teacher's performance
d. _____

ASSISTING THE SUPERVISING TEACHER: **A Relationship of Peers**

Both supervising teacher and college supervisor bring knowledge and insight into the student teaching situation. The supervising teacher possesses an intimate knowledge of the school and of the pupils; the college supervisor provides an increased understanding of the student teacher and of the responsibilities of student teaching. Both parties can benefit if they work together. An initial function of the college supervisor is to acquaint the supervising teacher with the nature of the university student teaching program. He can help a teacher understand his role and cause him to feel less apprehensive about his supervisory obligations.

Prior to, or early in the student teaching experience, the college supervisor and supervising teacher will probably consider the following topics:

The basic rationale of the student teaching program
    Philosophy
    Underlying principles
    Objectives of student teaching
The college and state requirements
    Number of hours to be taught
    Observation requirements
    Forms which are to be completed
    Reports and the dates they are due
    Amount of time the student teacher is to be in the school
    Types of activities the student teacher should experience
    Conferences
    Plans
    Evaluation and grading
Information about the student teacher
    Academic record
    Personal information
    Particular qualities
    Potential difficulties
Basic concepts of supervision
Role of the teacher education institution

It is beneficial for the college supervisor to be informed of the general nature of the school so that he may be aware of the particular challenges or opportunities facing the student teacher. If he is informed about the following, he may be in a better position to offer assistance:

The general nature of the content which the student teacher will teach
The general profile of the class or classes
    Unique characteristics
    Intelligence range
    Academic background
    Classroom personality
Established routines and procedures
Special projects or activities
General teaching procedure utilized
Available resource materials

The next contact with the college supervisor will probably occur a few weeks later when he makes a supervisory visit. During this time he will likely observe the student teacher as he teaches and conduct an extensive conference with him in regard to his experience. He will solicit the supervising teacher's analysis and will want to talk privately with him if possible. In addition to securing the information he desires, he can be of assistance to the supervising teacher by:

Suggesting additional experiences for the student teacher
Summarizing the student teacher's progress from a different perspective
Suggesting alternative procedures in
  Conferences
  Planning
  Working with students
Reviewing requirements and seeing that the university standards and state regulations are met
Counseling student teachers who are having problems
Serving as a liaison person between the student teacher and supervising teacher

The visit of the college supervisor may provide an opportunity for him to utilize his professional talents for the benefit of the specific teaching environment. He may be able to provide knowledge and information in regard to such areas as:

Latest developments in educational programs
Teaching skills
Resource materials
New techniques of instruction
Information about the college and teaching programs

The college supervisor can help the student teacher and enrich the school program if he is regarded as a peer in the professional education program. His contacts with other schools and other professionals help him to give a comprehensive perspective on educational affairs. Since his visits with schools provide experiences which cultivate his own background, he will be anxious to learn as well as to assist in professional concerns.

Case Study No. 25: THE COLLEGE SUPERVISOR EXPRESSES A POINT OF VIEW WHICH IS CONTRARY TO THE SUPERVISING TEACHER'S POLICY

In the course of your discussion with the college supervisor, he makes some observations concerning his beliefs about educational practice. He then asks questions in regard to your intended procedures in working with the student teacher. You have the impression that what you believe conflicts with his philosophy. You tend to feel rather strongly that you are correct and that you should follow the procedure as you had originally planned. How do you respond to his questions?

1. Explain your point of view and indicate your intent to proceed as you wish
2. Discuss the two different viewpoints and attempt to reconcile them into a policy which both of you can support
3. Attempt to conceal your view, but proceed as you wish
4. Attempt to conceal your view and follow his recommendations
5. Explain the difference to the student teacher and permit him to decide
6. _____

   Consider:

   a. Who has ultimate authority and responsibility in regard to the question being discussed
   b. The significance of the implications of the differing views
   c. The value of an exchange of views
   d. _____

The conference with the college supervisor developed in an easy, informal manner. Dr. Phillips asked questions which assessed the nature of the student teacher's progress as well as his meeting certification requirements. He was particularly interested in the amount of responsibility the student teacher was assuming, and he suggested a few teaching procedures which might be utilized. He answered Miss Bennett's questions and discussed a few ideas about evaluation that might be used for more effective analysis of Brian's teaching.

Brian came by after he had completed some prior commitments. After a discussion of his progress, Brian and Dr. Phillips explored plans for future goals and tasks. Dr. Phillips suggested that planning should be more thorough and that Brian should spend a little more time observing other teachers, concentrating on the analysis of the moves that seemed to make them successful. In response to one of Brian's questions, Dr. Phillips presented a rather detailed explanation of the technique of reflection through written records and analysis. Brian took out a pen and scribbled a few notes in the margin of his lesson plan and made a few entries in his student teaching journal. Miss Bennett silently mused over the change in Brian's reaction after he had experienced a real professional contact with his college supervisor.

Remember:

The college supervisor possesses expertise which should be utilized by both supervising teacher and student teacher

The college supervisor is in a position to assist in problems and difficulties - he should be contacted when he is needed

The college supervisor is concerned with the improvement of educational practice

The supervising teacher should cooperate and consult with the college supervisor, not only on problems of supervision, but also on classroom problems and methods

The college supervisor cannot perform his job properly if supervising teachers and student teachers have an erroneous conception of his duty

The college supervisor is a guide, confidant, and troubleshooter - utilize all needed roles

The college supervisor cannot assist if he does not know - inform him of the student teacher's activities in detail

The college supervisor is not primarily an evaluator during his supervisory visits; his role is to help the student develop into a better beginning teacher

USEFUL REFERENCES

ASSOCIATION FOR STUDENT TEACHING, *The College Supervisor: Conflict and Challenge,* Association for Student Teaching Yearbook, 1964, 237 pp.
　　Common concerns of college supervisors
　　Responsibilities of college supervisors
　　Guidelines

ASSOCIATION FOR STUDENT TEACHING, *The College Supervisor: Standards for Selection and Function,* Association for Student Teaching, 1968, 16 pp.
　　Selection of college supervisors
　　Guidelines for college supervisors

HANKE, DALE, "The College Supervisor: The Unsung Hero," *Teachers College Journal* 39:35-37, October, 1967
　　Responsibilities of the college supervisor
　　Personal relations
　　Nature of the position

INLOW, GAIL M., "The Complex Role of the College Supervisor," *Educational Research Bulletin* 35:10-17, January, 1956
　　Role of the college supervisor

NEAL, CHARLES D., KRAFT, LEONARD E., AND KRACHT, CONRAD R., "Reasons for College Supervision of the Student Teaching Programs," *Journal of Teacher Education* 18:24-27, Spring, 1967
　　Roles of the college supervisor

TANRUTHER, EDGAR M., *Clinical Experiences in Teaching for the Student Teacher or Intern,* Dodd, Mead and Co., 1968, Chapter 3
　　The teacher development team

Chapter Five

SUPERVISING OBSERVATIONS

Brian came into Miss Bennett's room and happily announced that he had just finished his last observation. Miss Bennett appeared somewhat surprised and asked, "But you still have four weeks left in student teaching. Are you certain you have completed all of them?"

"Oh yes, I have been keeping record," explained Brian. "I started early and observed frequently so that I could get them over with. What a relief! The teachers I observed are all right, but I get bored just sitting in a classroom."

Miss Bennett protested mildly, "But there is value in observing. Are you certain you want to finish just yet?"

Brian's answer was definite. "I learn more when I am teaching than I do watching someone else. I wish the university would be more practical and dispense with some of its 'Mickey Mouse' requirements. Now I can devote my time to organization and teaching. If you want me to assume some additional teaching, let me know. I have time for it now that observations are out of the way."

Miss Bennett, who was not quite prepared for this candid reaction about observations, started to reply when the warning bell sounded, signaling that class was due to begin in five minutes. This was beneficial in a way because she was not certain that she could adequately respond to Brian's negative feelings at this moment. Now she would have the opportunity to find out more about observations before she finalized this matter with him. . .

OBSERVATIONS: **Learning by Looking**

Observation is a common form of learning which is employed widely in many different professional studies. It is an efficient and, sometimes, the only method of exposing beginners to the more experienced practitioners. Seeing a task performed can be much more vivid than reading or hearing about it. As young professionals, student teachers are in need of contact with experienced teachers who exemplify excellence in their work. Ironically, it is this very fact that may cause the student teacher to initially resist observation. He often feels that his task is to demonstrate teaching competency rather than learn about teaching, and he may possess the mistaken notion that he is already expected to be familiar with all the different techniques and methods of teaching. The supervising teacher, being a more mature professional, has the responsibility of proving that a contact with the skilled members in the profession is a necessary and worthwhile learning procedure for the student teacher.

Observation of inexperienced or ineffective teachers can sometimes be worthwhile if the proper context is provided. If a student observes master teachers only, he may come to assume that his own performance is quite inadequate. Observations of teachers who have some problems may help the student teacher learn that his teaching is quite satisfactory. More careful analysis is called for in regard to observation of less effective teachers for at least two reasons: first, a student teacher may assume that the class is poor and he may tend to feel sorry for the teacher because he has to work with such difficult children. In this instance, a supervisor will need to tactfully help the student teacher examine the dynamics of the class in order to view the actual causes. Secondly, the supervising teacher will need to avoid making the direct accusation that the teacher is being displayed as "Exhibit A" of ineffective teaching. This person may already be sensitive and can resent being used as an example of poor teaching if he knows of it.

Observation is a broadening experience in several ways. In the first place, the student teacher has probably become more specialized as he has progressed through college and this new environment may be the first setting he has had for some time where he can see what other levels and other areas of study are like. The observation procedure is beneficial as well in the area of teaching technique in that a student teacher can be exposed to many different teaching styles and philosophies as he watches teachers in action. Finally, a good schedule of observations provides an opportunity for acquaintance with larger cross sections of the student body. Even seeing the same student in two different classes can be a very profitable experience.

Observations often are negatively associated with inactivity which most student teachers abhor. A student teacher is likely to accept observations more readily when he perceives that they can reveal possible answers to questions that are of prime interest to him. The challenge is to provide observation experiences where student teachers are convinced that they can learn something. If they perceive that such observations can help them become better teachers, they will give them higher priority on their schedules.

Most teacher-education institutions require their student teachers to complete some observations of other teachers as a prerequisite for recommendation for certification. The following benefits are most generally revealed through observations:

Orientation to the teaching environment where the student teacher will be working
  Management techniques and classroom routine
  Awareness of the supervising teacher's style
  Understanding of how pupils react to stimuli
  Knowledge of content and method
  Exposure to the problems of teaching
Learn additional teaching techniques
  Techniques of arousing student interest
  Identify skills which the student teacher can use in his own teaching
  Learn what makes "good" teaching effective
  Analyze teaching behavior which seems to be ineffective

*Provide a more comprehensive background for the consideration and
   evaluation of ideas and practices*
✓*Learn to evaluate teaching*
   Determining basic principles associated with teaching
   Recognizing theoretical implications
   Formulating a valid concept of what constitutes effective teaching
Gain a more comprehensive understanding of students
   Comparison of the same student in various school situations
   Understanding of the forces that determine student behavior
   Case study of special students
Gain a more comprehensive picture of the function of the school
   Other grade levels and other subjects taught
   Learning experiences which have preceded the student teacher's
      grade level
   Experiences which will follow the student teacher's grade level
   Relationship of various content areas to one another
   Curricula in the school
Identify teaching needs
   Needs of the student teacher
   Needs of the pupils
   Needs of the school
   Needs of the profession

Case Study No. 26: THE STUDENT TEACHER IS RELUCTANT
TO OBSERVE OUTSIDE HIS AREA OF INTEREST

   Your student teacher possesses a great deal of enthusiasm
for teaching. The only difficulty you have had with him is that he
does not want to spend time observing in other areas. He has
defended himself with the statement that he does not intend to
teach in those other areas, so he thinks it would be useless to
spend time observing them. How do you react to this?

1. Point out how he can improve his teaching by observing
   other selected classes
2. Specify that he must adhere to university requirements
   regardless of his feelings
3. Ask some other teachers to invite him to observe
4. Ask him to make a specific observation to see what he
   can learn
5. ————————————————————————

   Consider:

   a. Reasons for the student teacher's desire not to ob-
      serve
   b. Techniques of relating the student teacher's in-
      terests to observations
   c. ————————————————————

Case Study No. 27: THE STUDENT TEACHER CRITICIZES A TEACHER HE OBSERVES

Your student teacher has just observed a teacher who is generally regarded as somewhat ineffective. He greets you with the comment that it was the worst class he has ever seen. He continues to criticize thoroughly every aspect of the teacher's procedure. You suspect that most of his comments are accurate, but you wonder how you can approach the discussion of the observation and still remain ethical. What course of action do you pursue?

1. Confess that you wanted him to see the class in order to see what he obviously had viewed, and then admonish the student teacher to keep his thoughts confidential
2. Analyze the points mentioned in detail so that he can objectively appraise the class with a valid frame of reference as a guide
3. Caution him not to be too quick in making judgments or too outspoken with his criticisms
4. Ask him what he would have done if he had been the teacher in that situation.
5. _____

Consider:

a. The value of observing questionable teaching techniques
b. Professional ethics, including responsibilities both to the student teacher and the teacher who was observed
c. Structuring observation plans so the student can remain objective and analytical instead of evaluative
d. _____

SCHEDULING AND EXECUTING OBSERVATIONS: **Precision Should Prevail**

Observations are designed to achieve many different purposes. In order to meet these objectives, observations need to be scheduled at various times beginning the initial week and continuing through the concluding days of student teaching. The developmental pattern of the student teacher is such that his perceptions while observing teaching will be different at various times due to his expanded contact with pedagogy.

Early observations are likely to be dominated by a student teacher's concern for self and the environment where he will be teaching. How will he fit in? What are the pupils like whom he will be teaching? What is his supervising teacher's style? How does the supervising teacher manage to fill in a block of time? Well-structured observations during these early days can help orient the student teacher to the total school setting. Additionally, these early observations should provide some basis for his understanding of classroom dynamics and for the inauguration of his own teaching.

After he has had the experience of teaching children, he may consider observations as devices for the improvement of his own technique. An observation of a teacher may suggest some ideas which he can adapt to his own instructional style. If he is perceptive, he may begin to understand how certain teaching behaviors may accomplish desired results in class. He may learn that he can overcome some of his problems by observing the strengths of others. These midpoint observations can provide helpful information about his pupils as he observes them in other learning environments.

As the student teacher nears the completion of his tenure at the school, he should have formulated a more comprehensive outlook about teaching. He may now view education in more scientific terms and his understanding of the critical role of the teacher in creating effective learning should be more apparent. Observation at this time will cause him to look in more depth and achieve greater perception. Viewing teachers who are considered good, mediocre, or poor can assist him in developing a valid concept of good teaching.

If the student teacher fails to observe at any phase of his experience, he will have missed valuable opportunities which are necessary for complete development. Cramming observations into any brief period of the total student teaching experience is to deny the student teacher an opportunity to learn as much as he can from student teaching. The student teacher's concept of what to look for may be vague at all three levels of the experience unless the supervising teacher provides some direction. Observation of a teacher may seem trivial unless a student teacher knows what can be achieved for his direct benefit. The anecdotal records of nearly every college contain examples of a student teacher who went to sleep while observing or appeared so bored that the teacher asked the supervising teacher not to let him visit in any more of his classes.

The observation actually begins with the arrangement for the visit. Some teachers are quite conscious of the presence of an observer in the classroom, and they should be approached in a manner which indicates that the student teacher does not take this visit casually. The student teacher who makes arrangements in advance can expect more from the observation than the one who simply walks into the class to observe. His observation time may be utilized more efficiently since this procedure gives a teacher an opportunity to structure the class so that it has more relevance to the observer. It allows the teacher to plan to make certain learning features more discernible, and reduces the probability that the student teacher will spend most of his time observing a test or a supervised study period. Additionally, it should also be recognized that an advance arrangement can be less disturbing to the teacher than the last-minute arrival of the observer. Consequently, the teacher will be in better command of himself and give a better projection of his style.

Arrangements for observations are made by the student teacher, supervising teacher, department chairman, or administrator, depending upon the school. The student teacher should learn the procedure of his particular school and then follow that policy. Some schools operate on an informal basis while others require that requests be more formal. A typical formal request is indicated by the worksheet below.

Worksheet No. 4: A STUDENT TEACHER VISITATION REQUEST

TO: _____

FROM: _____

RE: Permission for Student Teacher to Visit Your Class

WHEN: Date _____   Class _____

       Period_____
       or hr.

       _____ Student Teacher
       _____ Supervising Teacher

If the above time is satisfactory, will you please sign and return one copy to the supervising teacher and keep the other copy for your records.

        Sign here for approval _____

Once the observation is arranged, a frame of reference can be developed which will make the observation more valid. Explanation of the context by the classroom teacher can mean the difference between a boring period of observation and a profitable opportunity. One reason an observation can be so uninteresting is that the student teacher has little or no concept of what he is to look for. Students seem to profit most from those observations which concentrate on some specific skill or idea. A student teacher who realizes that he is to note a teacher's style of interrogation will gain more from the experience than the one who is only instructed to observe to see what he can learn. If a supervising teacher is acquainted with the teaching style of the teacher to be observed, he will be performing a service for the student teacher if he points this out. Sometimes the supervising teacher may simply want the student teacher to compare the performance of one or more of his pupils in a different class. This, too, can have more meaning if the student teacher is aware of what to look for.

The student teacher should arrive in the room where he is to observe early enough to allow for any preliminary discussion or orientation which the teacher desires to make. Explanation of what is going to occur can encourage a student teacher to take more meaningful note of the classroom procedure. His early arrival also insures that he will not interrupt the activity by having to be seated after the class has already started.

The teacher will undoubtedly take note of the observer's reactions from time to time. Thus, the student teacher should be cued to display an active interest in the class. If he appears bored or indifferent, negative feelings can develop. The observer should show that he is genuinely interested in the work of the class.

An observation is not completed with the conclusion of a lesson. Since the observer is a guest, he should make a point to thank the teacher for permission to visit. The teacher may want to make a few comments about the procedure or even solicit the observer's reactions to the class. A few constructive comments by the student teacher are always in order. The teacher who observes the student teacher hastily making his way to the door following an observation may be either aggravated or disappointed. The student teacher's reactions to a class can affect a teacher's receptiveness to further observations by other student teachers.

The experience of an observation concludes with a discussion between the supervising teacher and the student teacher concerning what was learned. This discussion can lead to a very productive analysis of teaching techniques providing the conversation does not degenerate into a discussion of personality. Questions are good techniques for encouraging the student teacher to reflect on what he has observed.

The results of the observation should be apparent in the student teacher's later teaching style. If he has really learned from the observation, he may modify his teaching procedure, though it be ever so slight, toward improved instruction. Actual modification of teaching following an observation will depend upon the attitude of the observer, timing of the observation, development of observational criteria, and application of what has been learned to the observer's own specific teaching situation. The value of an hour's observation is often greater than an additional hour of teaching providing it is properly considered as a procedure for instructional improvement.

The supervising teacher's responsibilities concerning observations run concurrent with those of the student teacher, and a team approach is called for. If a student teacher has not been in contact with his supervisor in regard to observational procedures, his benefits from this aspect of his experience will be limited. The supervising teacher should be directly involved in helping the student teacher learn from observation experiences. Generally, his responsibilities are summarized as follows:

Set up the process for making observations outside his classroom
    Arrange a tentative pattern of observations
    Assist the student teacher in scheduling observations
Prepare the student teacher for the observation
    Describe the dynamics of the situation to be observed
    Indicate what might be learned in the class
Arrange for observations which fit the student teacher's particular readiness
Provide for observation of various types of teaching situations
    Both quality and less competent teaching
    Academically talented classes and less gifted groups
    Different types of educational programs within the school
    Teachers with differing philosophies of education
Help the student teacher analyze and evaluate what he has observed
    Discuss significant activities
    Determine what was learned

Case Study No. 28: THE STUDENT TEACHER FAILS TO LEARN FROM HIS OBSERVATIONS

    You began having your student teacher observe other classes after the first two weeks that he was in the school. Since he had started working as a teacher himself, you were convinced that he would gain several ideas from the various teachers he would see. Your inquiries only seem to bring vague responses and a rather indifferent attitude toward the teaching styles of the teachers he has seen. Furthermore, there has been no evidence of his having made any changes in his own procedure as a result of his having visited other classrooms. Since you are concerned about this, what course of action do you take?

1. Suggest that he discontinue observations for a few days
2. Structure the observations so that he will know what to look for
3. Cue the teacher to discuss the class with him
4. Ask the student teacher to take notes on the observation or to write a brief summary of his visit
5. Conduct a follow-up conference on the observation
6. Attempt to arrange the next few observations with the most interesting teachers you can find
7. ───────────────────────────────────

    Consider:

    a. The nature of the orientation for the observation
    b. Your attitude toward observation
    c. ─────────────────────────

Brian entered the teachers' work room with a list of notes and a look of anticipation on his face. He had just come from an observation of one of the more highly recognized teachers in the building.

"That class of Mr. Henson's is everything you said it was--and more. I really enjoyed watching him teach. I picked up two or three ideas that I can use next week with my class. Time went by so quickly that I had difficulty realizing that I had been there for an hour. He even got me involved in the discussion."

Miss Bennett resisted the temptation to remind him of his previous critical attitude toward observations and simply commented, "I thought you would enjoy seeing him. Now, what did you notice about the way he aroused student interest?"

Remember:

The supervising teacher should guide the student teacher in choosing observations and in reflecting upon them

In many situations observation is the most efficient method of learning about teaching

Observations will be more meaningful if adequate preparation is made

An observation will be worthwhile in proportion to the analysis provided at its conclusion

Observations are not requirements to "get out of the way" - they are techniques for learning certain professional skills

Observations can provide opportunities for reflection on the nature of one's own teaching

USEFUL REFERENCES

DEVOR, JOHN W., *The Experience of Student Teaching,* Macmillan Co., 1964, Chapter 3
Observation: physical, personnel, instructional, and management characteristics

MICHIGAN STATE UNIVERSITY, *Handbook for Supervising Teachers,* College of Education, Michigan State University, 1968, Chapter 5
Observing the teaching process

MURPHY, GERALDINE, "The Prospective Teacher as Observer," *Journal of Teacher Education* 13:150-156, June, 1962

SHARPE, DONALD M., *A Brief Guide to Secondary Student Teaching,* Indiana State University, Terre Haute, Indiana, 1970, pp. 22-23
Suggestions for planning and analyzing observations

STRATEMEYER, FLORENCE, AND LINDSEY, MARGARET, *Working with Student Teachers,* Teachers College Press, Columbia University, New York, 1958, Chapter 13
Purposes of observation
Principles in guiding student teachers in observations
Cooperative evaluation of the teaching-learning situation observed

Chapter Six

HELPING THE STUDENT TEACHER PLAN

Brian had now been well accepted in the school and seemed to be gaining confidence daily as he participated in more activities and assumed additional teaching obligations. He was becoming acquainted with teachers and had adjusted to the school routine very readily. His work with the class had been satisfactory, and he was scheduled to assume his maximum recommended teaching load within a few days. He had been working diligently on his lesson plans and was seen poring over a recent college textbook and consulting the planning section of his student teaching guide.

Miss Bennett assumed that Brian would consult with her about his teaching ideas, but he had not made any reference to his plans since she assigned the unit for him to teach and gave him the course of study and a list of possible resources. Several days elapsed and she had seen none of his planning nor had he discussed any ideas with her. She wanted to see his plans in their present form so that she could be certain that he was making constructive progress, and she wondered how much suggestion she should make once she did see the ideas that he was developing.

Miss Bennett finally decided to cautiously approach the subject with her student teacher. At the beginning of their conference, she attempted to smile casually and said, "Four more days and you will have full responsibility for the class. Do you have your ideas worked out?"

Brian shuffled some papers and looked at her in an uncertain manner . . .

REQUIRED PLANS: **Valuable Tools, Necessary Evils, or Busy Work?**

The concept of effective planning is difficult for a student teacher to comprehend. The plans which he may have previously constructed in college courses were probably content centered and almost certainly unrelated to any specific teaching situation. The mechanics may have been stressed more than content or usefulness as a teaching tool. Once he arrives at the school, the student teacher often observes that the supervising teacher does an excellent bit of teaching without any "plan" in front of him.

Planning may be outlining topics or it may simply be "having something to do every minute of the hour" as far as the student teacher is concerned. It is not uncommon for a student teacher to classify planning as busy work because it seems to involve a lot of useless writing which really is not related to the immediate teaching problem as perceived by the student teacher. The broad concept of planning may have escaped him entirely.

A major task for the supervising teacher is communication concerning the real nature of planning. Inexperience or insecurity may cause a student teacher to be hesitant in preparing thorough plans. On the other hand, a willing student teacher may not plan adequately because he does not understand what is expected of him. The student teacher should have the responsibility of making some decisions about the nature of both content and teaching process. Otherwise, he will simply be participating in a mechanical procedure which appears to be a routine of trivia. Individual subjects as well as school policy will determine the extent of such latitude. The supervising teacher should clearly explain the guidelines that he expects the student teacher to follow in formulating his plans.

It is probably more important to focus on the process of planning rather than upon the form in which plans are to be prepared. The student teacher may have to be convinced of the value of planning as a procedure for effecting better teaching. He should come to know that a good plan, written or unwritten, has considered the basic objectives, content, procedure, and evaluation of a lesson or unit. The form will become logical as he conceptualizes the real function of planning.

The supervising teacher has the right to expect a student teacher to prepare both long-range and daily plans, but he has to help the student teacher learn to prepare, especially in the early phases of teaching. The student teacher's attempts at planning have probably been in the abstract. Now this real situation demands that plans be organized in such a way that they will actually assist him in good teaching.

Planning should be required which will achieve the following results:

The student teacher will have stature as a partner in the teaching-learning process

The planning process will be an experience which is designed to assist in thinking through objectives and deciding which teaching techniques will best meet those objectives

The plan will provide security in working with a class

The plan will serve as a guide to insure an effective learning environment

The plan will offer the supervising teacher an opportunity to make suggestions prior to presentation that will result in more effective instruction

The completed plan will be a guide which can be used in the analysis of a lesson

A successful plan with adaption can be used with another group of students

There is no one type of plan which can be prescribed for a student teacher. The form and detail are determined by such factors as type of subject matter, the need of the individual who will use it, the activity of the lesson, and the nature of the class which is to be taught. The supervising teacher should encourage the student teacher to experiment with various types of planning so that he can determine the procedure which proves best for him to follow and which is best for various types of classroom situations. Agreement should be made upon the following points:

The form plans are to take
How far in advance of presentation plans are to be submitted for review
   by the supervising teacher
The amount of detail that should be written into the plan

The supervising teacher should assist the student teacher in making and using lesson plans that are suitable to the subject, to the situation, and to the student teacher's own personal style. A student teacher may be inclined to go from day to day doing whatever appears immediately desirable or important. He may need to be helped to verbalize what he is trying to do, how it fits into what has already been done, and how it leads to what is to follow. The supervisor may give his best help by asking questions. In answering the questions, the student teacher should become aware of the structure of his subject and his thought, permitting himself to carry out his daily work on a more meaningful basis.

Case Study No. 29: AN INADEQUATE CONCEPT OF PLANNING

You have had several discussions with your student teacher concerning planning. On each occasion she has seemed to indicate that plans constitute unnecessary burdens and that she cannot teach if she has to constantly check what is written on a piece of paper. You have indicated that you would like to see some evidence of detailed planning for the first unit. She presents it to you with the question, "Is that what you want?" How do you respond?

1. "Is this what you think you need?"
2. "Yes, if it covers objectives, content, procedures, and evaluation."
3. "That can only be answered after you have taught the lesson."
4. "My wants are based on the need for you to think through what is to occur. I need to know what you are thinking so that I can see how the lesson will be executed."
5. _____

Consider:

a. A method by which you can communicate the essence of planning
b. The basic essentials of preparation
c. The reason for the student teacher's doubts about the value of preparation
d. _____

Case Study No. 30: THE STUDENT TEACHER PRESENTS NO WRITTEN PLANS

You have a seemingly confident student teacher. In spite of your efforts, he has not produced any written material. His teaching has been acceptable, but you are aware that his development would be much better if you could talk with him in advance concerning his proposed class procedures. On Monday morning you ask him if he has his plans for the week. He casually remarks that he does not bother with writing anything down because it is all in his mind. Since you feel that analysis is important. what do you do to get written plans?

1. Indicate that you will cease to ask for thorough plans when he demonstrates that he can teach well
2. Allow him to discover the need for planning by permitting him to teach when he is not prepared
3. Refuse to let him teach until the required plans are produced
4. Extensively analyze his lessons and indicate where he could have done better if he had thought through the lesson more thoroughly or shared his ideas with you
5. ꞌAsk the college supervisor to clarify the university position in regard to required lesson plans
6. _____

Consider:

a. The impact upon the pupils
b. Procedures which communicate the value of your point of view
c. A common position that might be acceptable to both student teacher and supervising teacher
d. _____

Case Study No. 31: CONSIDERING THE POOR LESSON PLAN

Your student teacher has just submitted his plan for the next class. You were aware that he has presented a design that obviously would not be effective. Since you realize its limitations and your student teacher does not, what course of action do you pursue?

1. Wait until he teaches the class and then discuss the reasons for lack of success after the class has been taught
2. Confer in advance and help him devise a better plan
3. Be prepared to assist the student teacher when he teaches the class
4. _____

Consider:

a. The effect of the lesson upon the class
b. The effect of each of the alternatives upon the student teacher
c. 'One generally learns better from success than from failure
d. ———————————————————————

ADVANCE PLANNING: **One Week or One Hour?**

Student teachers who plan in advance seem to perform better than those who do not. Those who prepare on a last-minute schedule find that deadlines are always harassing them and that some of their hasty decisions may cause unfortunate results. Advance organization provides opportunity for analysis and revision before teaching occurs. Sequences can be more orderly because the teacher is familiar with the total pattern of activities.

Final decisions concerning some plans may have to be delayed until a previous lesson has been taught because the rate of progress cannot be determined. Nearly every plan may need some last-minute revision on the basis of the previous class activity. In spite of this, the basic operating procedure of planning as far in advance as possible appears just as appropriate for student teachers as it does for experienced teachers. Plans ought to be ready far enough ahead so that effective organization for teaching is insured. Certain factors determine the format of advance planning. These points have to be assessed in determining the nature of advance preparation:

The necessity of advance planning for a particular class or unit
   A field trip or laboratory may require several days' organization
   A sequential lesson may have to wait until the previous one is completed to determine how much progress has been made or to determine specific needs for the next lesson
The progress of the student teacher
   If progress is satisfactory, the supervisor may find it necessary to see plans only a short while before the class is taught
   A student whose progress is slow may need to have plans reviewed in detail before teaching--perhaps as much as a day or two earlier
The amount of preparation which would be involved
   Reading
   Preparation of illustrative materials
   Securing media

The ability of the student to think in long-range terms
Time available for preparation
Availability of physical resources for planning

Every effort should be made to see that plans are presented far enough ahead of time so that necessary revision can occur prior to teaching. This deadline should be governed by standards that are realistic. Asking student teachers, particularly new ones, to prepare daily plans for a week in advance could pose an almost impossible task. Requirements for a great amount of unnecessary written work in planning can also prove to be an excessive task for some student teachers.

Case Study No. 32: THE PLANS ARE PRODUCED AT THE LAST MINUTE

Your student teacher always has her plans, but they come to you close to the actual time the class is to be taught. Because of this, you only have time to review them briefly before the class begins. Obviously, this leaves no time for revision. Since you feel that the procedure is of relatively little value to you, you would like to see the plans earlier. How do you go about getting her to submit the plans when you want them?

1. Specifically ask her to have the plans for you a certain number of days in advance
2. Confer with her about the process which causes her to be so late in submitting plans
3. Deliberately discuss future lessons and explore the ideas verbally ahead of time
4. _____

   Consider:

   a. Reasons for the late submission of plans
   b. The effect of the late submission upon success in the classroom
   c. Whether the standards and requirements are realistic
   d. _____

Case Study No. 33: TOO MUCH ADVANCE PLANNING

There are times when you wish your student teacher would plan less. She always enters class with a stack of books and a comprehensive, well-typed plan. Everything is written out in detail. Obviously this consumes a lot of time and its effect is indicated in the lack of vitality and neglect of some of the other requirements of student teaching. The overemphasis on formal planning may be destroying her objective of good teaching in that she relies too much on her plans and lacks a sense of timing and enthusiasm in presentation. How do you go about correcting this situation?

1. Explain that you do not want such detailed planning
2. Discuss the plans with her and attempt to help her see what parts are necessary as well as what features are not as important for lesson execution
3. Suggest activities which she might pursue which would not require so much thorough organization
4. Tape record a session and then discuss the qualities that are lacking from the class, hoping this will lead to acceptance of reorganized procedures
5. ——————————————————————————

Consider:

a. The reason for the fact that the student teacher devotes so much time to the mechanics of planning
b. Emphasis on ideas and techniques instead of written plans
c. ——————————————————————

Case Study No. 34: THE STUDENT TEACHER IS UNPREPARED FOR AN ASSIGNED CLASS

Linda asked if you would like to have additional time today to teach your unit. You submit that she will not have time to teach her unit if you take more time, but she explains that she is perfectly willing to let it carry over until tomorrow. Although you do not understand her reluctance to teach, you comply and complete your unit with the benefit of the additional period of time. Linda, of course, then has no time to teach that day.

As the two of you walk to the parking lot at the end of the day, Linda casually comments that she had not been prepared to teach the section which had been assigned to her because her fiance had come by last night and they went to a movie. You now understand her motive in offering to give you more time to teach.

What do you do in this situation?

1. Resolve that you will always review plans at least one day in advance
2. Determine that you will not yield to such a request again
3. Plan a conference with Linda and focus on the necessity of meeting responsibilities
4. Dismiss the incident as an isolated situation which will probably not recur.
5. ——————————————————————————

Consider:

a. The implication upon the learning and attitude of the pupils
b. The effect of covering for a student teacher's lack of preparation
c. Procedures for systematic review of plans
d. ——————————————————————

SHARING PLANS AND RESOURCES WITH THE STUDENT TEACHER:
Opening the Confidential Files

Developing a lesson plan is a creative endeavor for a student teacher just as it is for a professional educator who has several years of experience. Creativity is based on knowledge, and the person who fashions a new invention has a thorough knowledge of his field before he has the perception and imagination to attempt fresh ways of doing things. A student teacher, with his limited background and experience, should be as familiar as possible with ideas for planning in order to be more creative. If he does not know alternatives, he may rely on less acceptable and less exciting types of planning. The study of different types of successful plans can help him produce more effective designs.

The supervising teacher is often reluctant to show his plans to the student teacher because he is concerned that the student teacher would simply tend to copy them rather than to devise his own teaching techniques. An insecure student teacher can be tempted to use his supervisor's plans verbatim and it is likewise tempting for a dominating teacher to encourage him to do so. Such a possibility can be avoided if the teacher presents his plans in a way that leads the student teacher to consider them as mere guidelines. Their strengths and limitations can be mentioned as the student teacher is encouraged to find the best way to prepare for a particular class. The sharing of plans can enrich the alternatives for a student teacher as he approaches the planning of a lesson.

The beginning student teacher will likely be unaware of the facilities and resources in the school and community which can be utilized in enriching a classroom. He should have the opportunity to learn about and utilize some or all of the resources described below:

Library resources
Audio-visual materials
    Films
    Filmstrips
    Recordings
    Tape recorders
    Video-tape-recorders
Available supplies and equipment
Resource consultants
Community resources
    Public library
    Service organizations
    Business and industry
Available funds for purchase of supplies or materials for instruction
Pupil talents

Publications available in quantity
Resource materials within the teacher's classroom
   Publications
   Bulletin board material
   Equipment
   Supplies

Such materials and ideas may have eluded the student teacher's consideration. If the student teacher realizes the value of these resources and learns of their availability, he will be more likely to plan creative activities himself instead of depending on the supervising teacher's plans or emulating other instructors.

Case Study No. 35: THE STUDENT TEACHER ATTEMPTS TO IMITATE THE SUPERVISING TEACHER

Each teacher has to develop his own style of teaching. A procedure that is perfect for one teacher may cause another to experience utter failure. You recognize this, but your student teacher has not yet been able to grasp this concept. Since you are a "master teacher" she is certain that whatever procedure you devise has to be superior to any of her techniques. Consequently, she observes you teach and then attempts to imitate your procedures. Instead of offering ideas for your approval, she asks for your ideas and plans and then attempts to follow them. Obviously she is experiencing little success and is becoming concerned about her ability to teach. What changes do you make to attempt to improve the situation?

1. Teach your class after the student teacher has taught, thus prohibiting imitation of the same lesson
2. Indicate that she has followed your pattern; now you are going to follow her plans for a while in order to learn some different procedures from the ones which you have used for some time
3. Ask for her ideas and techniques in planning conferences
4. Tactfully suggest that she observe other teachers for new ideas instead of constantly observing you
5. Explain why your procedures will not necessarily work for another teacher
6. Express confidence in the student teacher's ability to create her own plans
7. ——————————————————————

   Consider:

   a. The reason for the student teacher's penchant for conforming to your procedures
   b. Methods of illustrating that more than one approach to a topic is possible
   c. ————————————————————

Case Study No. 36: THE STUDENT TEACHER FAILS TO THOROUGHLY PLAN FOR A FIELD TRIP

At your suggestion your student teacher decided to plan a field trip to utilize some nearby resources which could enrich the class. Since he was inexperienced in contacts beyond the classroom, he is overlooking several details that will need to be attended to in order to insure that the trip will be successful. He has failed to check with the administration and his timing is going to be a problem if he proceeds according to his present schedule. He has not remembered to orient the pupils adequately or to remind them of their responsibilities. Since it is potentially a good project and you want it to be of value to him, what do you do?

1. Arrange for some of the details he has neglected without his knowledge
2. Inform him of the details he needs to take care of before the activity is inaugurated
3. Let him take complete control and discuss the activity after it has been completed
4. Be ready to assist when the obvious problems occur
5. _____

Consider:

a. The best procedure in making use of resources outside the classroom
b. The difficulty involved in arranging for utilization of resources outside the classroom
c. Responsibilities to the school, pupils, and resource personnel
d. Possible attitude of the student teacher toward field trips in the event that the first one would fail.
e. _____

The class had ended and Brian returned to the teachers' room where Miss Bennett had been working.

"How was the lesson?"

"Better than yesterday," Brian was quick to report. "I had plenty of examples this time and there were no lapses of time because there was not enough for them to do."

"How was the timing?"

"It seemed to be much better than before. I didn't stay with any one activity longer than fifteen minutes."

"I think that's best for this class," commented Miss Bennett.

Brian mentioned that Bill had asked him in class why they had to study all that 'stuff'.

Miss Bennett inquired, "What did you tell him?"

Brian relaxed, "I recalled that intensive examination you gave me yesterday in regard to objectives and explained why it was important, and he seemed to accept it. And I thought you were putting me on when you were interrogating me in regard to purposes."

"You cannot be too well prepared to teach that group," noted Miss Bennett. *"I have always felt that it is better to 'prevent' by good preparation than it is to 'remedy' by re-teaching."*

Brian instantly responded, *"I completely agree. If I had not planned for this lesson ahead of time, I would have been in a considerable amount of difficulty."*

Miss Bennett smiled as she closed her grade book. *"You are making real progress, Brian. Continue to thoroughly plan and you will prevent a lot of difficulties before they occur."*

Remember:

A well-developed lesson plan is a student teacher's best friend when teaching a class

Emphasis on results should prevail over emphasis on form

Every teacher plans - the process and extent differ with individuals

　　It is helpful for the student teacher to be familiar with the supervising teacher's process

Good planning depends on an adequate concept of purpose and a knowledge of the learning rate of pupils - this may be a new thought to a student teacher

The Association for Student Teaching recommends the following:[1]

　　Planning should be done cooperatively, with both supervising teacher and student teacher suggesting activities and ways of working with pupils

　　The supervising teacher should acquaint the student with his yearly plans, reviewing developments that occurred before the arrival of the student teacher and projecting developments that will likely occur after he leaves

　　The supervising teacher should explain his procedures for pupil-teacher planning

　　The supervising teacher should review the teaching plans made by the student teacher, raising appropriate questions and making helpful suggestions

　　The supervising teacher should provide evaluative sessions in which the student teacher gains skill in judging the effectiveness of his plan

　　The supervising teacher should make certain that the student teacher has submitted his plans for constructive criticism far enough in advance of the teaching commitment for the student teacher to revise plans as necessary, incorporating appropriate suggestions

　　The supervising teacher should project with the student teacher a sequence of varied responsibilities that will enable the student teacher to become involved gradually in all aspects of the program

1 Association for Student Teaching, **Guiding Student Teaching Experiences,** Bulletin No. 1, 1969, pp. 13-14.

The supervising teacher should encourage the student teacher to use his initiative and creativity by giving him the freedom, within acceptable limits, to initiate practices and procedures not customarily followed by the supervising teacher

USEFUL REFERENCES

ASSOCIATION FOR STUDENT TEACHING, *Guiding Student Teaching Experiences,* Association for Student Teaching Bulletin No. 1, pp. 12-14
    Guidance in planning
BATCHELDER, HOWARD T., McGLASSON, MAURICE, AND SCHORLING, RALEIGH, *Student Teaching in Secondary Schools,* McGraw-Hill, 1964, Chapter 7
    Teacher and pupils plan together
BROWN, THOMAS J., *Student Teaching in a Secondary School,* Harper and Row, 1960, Chapter 6
    How to plan a lesson
BYERS, LORETTA, AND IRISH, ELIZABETH, *Success in Student Teaching,* D. C. Heath and Co., 1961, Chapter 2
    Planning for teaching
CROW, LESTER D., AND CROW, ALICE, *The Student Teacher in the Elementary School,* David McKay Co., 1965, Chapters 6, 7
    Planning for effective teaching
    Planning in subject areas
    Planning the daily lesson
CURTIS, DWIGHT K., AND ANDREWS, L. O., *Guiding Your Student Teacher,* Prentice-Hall, 1954, Chapter 7
    Learning to plan
DEVOR, JOHN W., *The Experience of Student Teaching,* Macmillan Co., 1964, Chapter 6
    Planning your work
NELSON, LESLIE, AND McDONALD, BLANCHE, *Guide to Student Teaching,* Wm. C. Brown, 1958, Chapter 5
    Student teacher planning
OLIVA, PETER F., *The Secondary School Today,* World Publishing Company, 1967, Chapter 7
    Planning a learning unit
    Planning a lesson
POPHAM, JAMES W., AND BAKER, EVA L., *Systematic Instruction,* Prentice-Hall, 1970
STRATEMEYER, FLORENCE, AND LINDSEY, MARGARET, *Working with Student Teachers,* Teachers College Press, Columbia University, 1958, Chapter 9
    Guiding the student teacher in planning learning experiences
TANRUTHER, EDGAR, *Clinical Experiences in Teaching for the Student Teacher or Intern,* Dodd, Mead and Co., New York, 1967, Chapter 4
    Foundations for planning
    Planning with the supervising teacher
    Planning with pupils

Chapter Seven

GUIDING TEACHING

Elaine Bennett strolled into the teachers' lounge and was greeted by a group of teachers who were unaccustomed to seeing her in the room in the middle of the morning.

"Not teaching today?" inquired Martha Wilson, who normally has a break at this time.

"I am letting Mr. Sims teach the class this morning."

The "lounge lizards" were quick to go to work on her.

"Sure must be nice," volunteered Toni Bridges, a second-year teacher who had not yet acquired the knack of being well organized. "I wish I could have someone to do my work for me and be paid extra for it."

"Best thing you ever did," blurted Joe Hanley, who possessed a notorious reputation for abandoning his student teachers. "Shoulda left him after the second day. They can't teach while you're in the room. They need to be left by themselves. I tell my student teachers that they can find me here if they need me. Otherwise, I will know they are getting along all right. Gives 'em confidence to be left alone."

"Perhaps I'm from the old school, but I think we should not turn our classes over to a beginner." All eyes turned to Sylvia Rose, an institution in the Central City System. "I want to know what goes on in my classes, and the students these days will take advantage of a student teacher. Besides, you have to keep a close watch on some of these student teachers or they will be teaching some of that nonsense they are picking up at the university and indoctrinating our children with a lot of liberal tripe. A supervising teacher should be in the room all the time seeing that the student teacher is doing what he is supposed to do."

Miss Bennett frowned, "I was following Brian's wishes and what I understood was the desire of the university. He felt that he was ready to be left alone for a while. I think that he needs to have this kind of responsibility occasionally."

"Sure he does," boomed Hanley.

"I don't think you can help a student teacher if you do not know what is going on in the class," countered Miss Rose.

Toni Bridges interjected, "All I know is I wish I had the opportunity to use one in my class. I sure need the help."

Miss Bennett quickly finished her coffee, excused herself, and was last seen heading for the library where there was a study room which was usually vacant.

INDEPENDENT TEACHING EXPERIENCE: Those Fragile Solos

The task of providing effective supervision is one of the most complex tasks in working with student teachers. The supervising teacher's responsibilities must range from helping the student teacher achieve emotional independence in the classroom to analyzing and developing teaching strategies. Freedom must be permitted, yet responsibility has to be retained. This delicate balance ranges from assumption of classroom responsibility to the evaluation of the pupils.

The question of independent teaching experience is a concern of both supervising teachers and student teachers. The fact that the supervising teacher has the responsibility for the class may cause him to be reluctant to be absent with a beginner in charge. The student teacher's dilemma is that he may wish to have the teacher present for support in case it is needed; yet he may feel more comfortable when the teacher is not in the room during periods of instruction.

Complete professional development depends on the ability of a teacher to perform an act, study it, and plan a future course of action which benefits from the prior experience. Independent teaching is a necessary condition in this procedure in that it provides an actual encounter with the real classroom environment. The supervising teacher's indispensable role is to help the student teacher reflect upon the act, provide input of new information and thoughts, and guide in the formulation of a more comprehensive assessment or plan of action. The predominant goal in this process is the ability of the student teacher to be independent in both performing and analyzing the teaching act. In order to accomplish this aim, a great amount of discretion will have to be used in providing the proper experience at the correct time--a desirable portion of observed teaching and an adequate amount of independent practice.

The poorest procedure that a supervising teacher can follow is to leave the student teacher completely alone. This abandonment prevents him from receiving the anticipated benefit from supervisory observations. However, the practice of never leaving the student teacher alone with the class can be almost as damaging to his professional development. Either of these two extremes will not help the student teacher learn as he should. A student teacher needs to have the class by himself often enough to feel that he has personal responsibility for the direction of learning. This is necessary for the development of his confidence and of his unique teaching style. The supervising teacher must be in the room enough to observe the teaching skills of the student teacher and to help him improve and evaluate his work.

There is no formula which can be used in determining an absolute pattern for supervisory presence. A competent supervising teacher will be aware of the necessity of being cognizant of what is actually occurring in the classroom. This will be accomplished by different teachers in varying amounts of visitations depending upon the actual real communication that is established in understanding the student teacher's progress. This balance between complete classroom responsibility and observed supervision more commonly results when the supervising teacher is in the room approximately one-half of the time. The supervisory observations are more effective if they are conducted in a manner in which neither student teacher nor pupils can detect the supervisory pattern, i.e., in one day, out the next; visit the first part of the class, leave the last, or some other pattern which seems to be unpredictable. When the trend of supervisory observations cannot be detected, the supervising teacher will be able to observe the more typical situations.

The supervising teacher is normally needed in the room a greater percentage of the time during the first few weeks than during the last few weeks. Sometimes it is good practice to leave the student teacher alone for the entire day, but this should only be done when the supervising teacher is convinced that the student teacher has matured to the point where he can assume full responsibility for the class. The student teacher should know at all times where the supervising teacher can be found or where a responsible school official can be reached in case of need or emergency.

Case Study No. 37: DECIDING WHETHER TO OBSERVE THE STUDENT TEACHER'S FIRST SUSTAINED PERIOD OF TEACHING

It is the first day that your student teacher is to present a complete lesson to the class. Progress in cooperative teaching has been satisfactory, but she has never been tested by the challenge of a long presentation. She is understandably tense, and you want to support her as best you can. Unable to decide whether you should remain with the class or leave the room, you finally ask which alternative she prefers. She indicates that your being in the room will make her more nervous because she knows that you could do a much better job, but on the other hand, she fears that she does not know what she will do if "something happened."

Given this indication of her feelings, what do you decide to do?

1. Remain in the room
2. Remain in the room until you are convinced that her progress will be satisfactory and then leave
3. Remain in the room, but be preoccupied with some other activity so that you do not appear to be judging her performance
4. Leave the room, but let her know where you will be
5. Leave the room the first part of the class and return later to determine how she is progressing
6. Listen outside the classroom where neither the student teacher nor pupils know you are listening
7. ―――――――――――――――――――――――――――――――

Consider:

a. Methods of assuring the student teacher that performance will be satisfactory
b. The student teacher's reasons for uncertainty
c. The implications for both class and student teacher if the lesson should not be satisfactory
d. Techniques of preparing the class for the first presentation

e. Type of understanding and communication which has developed, between you and the student teacher

f. _____

Case Study No. 38: THE STUDENT TEACHER ASKS THE SUPERVISOR TO LEAVE THE ROOM SO THAT HE WILL BE MORE AT EASE

Your student teacher has had the responsibility of teaching one group of pupils for three days. His performance has not been very satisfactory, but you have reserved making any criticisms in order to give him an opportunity to develop confidence before you begin to help him strive for improvement. On the morning of the fourth day, he asks you if he might teach the class alone because he is self-conscious with you in the room and he feels that he might do better if he were left alone with the class. What action do you take?

1. Respect his wishes and leave while he is teaching
2. Indicate that you feel that he may not yet be ready to be left alone
3. Discuss his progress by reviewing his current difficulties and then indicate some methods of improving
4. _____

Consider:

a. Evaluative techniques that will cause the student teacher to solicit your suggestions
b. Techniques of building the student teacher's security and confidence
c. Procedures which will enable you to be in the class, but will not convey the feeling that you are being critical
d. The possible implications of delayed discussion of teaching progress
e. Whether the nature of the class or the content of the lesson are appropriate for the student teacher to begin teaching
f. _____

LEGAL STATUS: **Nobody's Child**

The legal status of student teachers in most states is not clearly defined by statute. In some cases there are neither definitive clarifications nor guidelines concerning the legal prerogatives of the student teacher. This is in contrast to a certified teacher's status which is defined by law in some detail. The legal position of the student teacher has become a point of concern recently in spite of the fact that litigation rarely occurs. Although most states require that student teaching must be completed before teacher certification is granted, the student teacher's legal position is generally rather precarious. He must student teach for certification, but he may not have any lawful basis for exercising his teaching responsibilities.

A few states have enacted legislation designed to clarify the legal status of student teachers. Although each law is different, the intention is usually to authorize teacher-education institutions and public schools to enter into agreements for the purpose of providing teaching experience for those who are preparing for the education profession. The typical law further states that a student teacher shall be given the same legal authority and status as a certified employee of the school district.

Legal provisions usually fail to clarify the role of the student teacher as a substitute for his supervising teacher. The position usually taken is that a student teacher may substitute for his supervising teacher for a day or two providing he has been in the school long enough to develop a reasonable degree of competency. Additional substitute work is generally considered to be an encroachment on his responsibilities as a student teacher. Substitute policies are normally formulated by the local school administration with concurrence of the univeristy.

Questions concerning the lawful status of a student teacher in the event of a professional day of protest or a strike are not covered by legislation, nor is there likely to be a policy which dictates a course of action. The condition of "non-involvement" seems to be the one most commonly accepted. If a supervising teacher is at work as a teacher, the student teacher can continue to teach his regular classes, but he may not substitute for an absent teacher. In the event the supervising teacher is absent, the student teacher is encouraged to remain away from the school or to return to the university for instructions. If there is any question of interpretation, the student teacher and his supervisor are advised to consult with the building principal or the university coordinator of student teaching.

A supervising teacher may desire clarification of legal roles and prerogatives before the student teacher arrives. In preparing for this, the following questions may serve to guide him in securing the most relevant information:

What is the legal status of student teachers in the state?
    Tort liability
    Administration of discipline
    Responsibility in areas where dangerous equipment is operating
      or potentially dangerous activity is conducted
What kind of legal protection is provided for the student teacher in the particular school?
    Does the school provide liability coverage for its student teachers?

*Who is responsible for the class if the student teacher is alone with the
  group?*
*In what situations may the student teacher legally and ethically be used
  as a substitute teacher?*
*What is the role of the student teacher in the event of a teacher strike or
  a day of professional protest?*
*Are there responsibilities a certified teacher cannot delegate to a
  student teacher?*
Can a student teacher administer corporal punishment?

The normal day-to-day work in a class presents no problem or difficulty as far as the student teacher's legal status is concerned. It is the considered professional opinion that courts will normally uphold a student teacher's legal status in the school because of the requirement of student teaching for certification; however, the profession is slowly attempting to further clarify the question of legal responsibility, and the supervising teacher should attempt to be aware of all laws and policies which relate to his teaching situation. The teacher who works with students in areas where injury is most likely to occur needs to be especially aware of such policies and regulations. Finally, the supervising teacher should remember that his classes are his moral and legal responsibility and not the responsibility of the student teacher.

Case Study No. 39: THE ROLE OF A STUDENT TEACHER IN A
DAY OF PROTEST

The teachers in your school district have decided to stage a professional day of protest in order to dramatize their needs and concerns. They have agreed to march in front of the building carrying signs describing their grievances. The school administration has announced that school will remain open by utilizing those teachers who are not protesting and by hiring substitutes. You have decided that you will report for your regular duty at school. The student teacher asks what he should do. What do you suggest?

1. Indicate that he should come to school and follow the same schedule that he has been pursuing
2. Suggest that he take all your classes thereby enabling you to substitute for an absent colleague
3. Suggest that he substitute in one of the classrooms which will be vacant
4. Ask him to seek direction from the principal
5. Suggest that he follow the dictates of his own conscience - come to school if he wishes, join those who are protesting, or return to campus for the day
6. Suggest that he consult with his college supervisor for instructions
7. _____

Consider:

a. Legal protection or lack of it
b. Possible legal actions that could be taken against the student teacher
c. Ethical standards related to this problem
d. Responsibility to pupils
e. _____

Case Study No. 40: DECIDING ON THE ADVISABILITY OF LEAVING A STUDENT TEACHER ALONE IN A CLASSROOM WHERE INJURY IS POSSIBLE

Several activities in your classroom are potentially dangerous if not properly supervised. The increased concern about liability has caused you to be careful in seeing that you could not be charged with negligence. This becomes a problem as you are aware of the need for the student teacher to develop his ability to direct a class by himself. What do you decide to do?

1. Leave him with the class but make certain that he understands all the safety precautions
2. Do not leave the room
3. Remain in the room but give the student teacher complete responsibility for part of the group
4. Ask for a legal interpretation before you decide
5. Leave him with the class, assuming that responsibility is of no significance in the decision
6. _____

Consider:

a. Legal status of the student teacher as it is interpreted by the school
b. Procedure to insure that a situation is completely safe
c. Implications of the student teacher's not assuming complete responsibility
d. _____

OBSERVING THE STUDENT TEACHER: **Necessary Intimidation**

The appearance of an observer in a classroom can be uncomfortable for an experienced teacher, and it can seem very threatening to the inexperienced student teacher. The presence of a visitor may cause a student teacher to be more tense and to have greater difficulty in performing to the best of his ability. Most student teachers will readily admit that they feel more comfortable when the supervising teacher is not present.

The necessity of observation is obvious. Evaluation or analysis cannot be effectively made unless the supervising teacher is aware of the actual situation. The experience of being observed also can be the beginning of self-analysis and of more open communication with other professionals. In spite of these admitted values, the problem remains that the student teacher can feel uneasy in a supervisor's presence in the classroom if he appears to be evaluating his teaching. The challenge confronting the supervising teacher is that of creating an environment which permits the student teacher to be natural while supervisory observations are conducted.

A logical beginning is to recognize the conditions which cause a student teacher to feel uncomfortable. The following situations are more likely to create uncertainty on the part of the student teacher when he is being observed:

A lack of thorough planning or uncertainty about the development of the lesson
A perception of inadequacy in fulfilling the expected role
A feeling that the observation is an "inspection"
Lack of understanding of the role of the observer
Too much writing by the observer, especially when such writing consists of notes that are not later shown to the student teacher
Facial expressions which convey disagreement, confusion, or boredom
Interruptions by the observer
Infrequent observations
Lack of constructive analysis on a continuous basis
    No pre-teaching conference concerning plans.
    No post-teaching analysis of performance
    Confrontations or arguments instead of conversation and dialogue

Specific suggestions for making observations less threatening can be inferred from the above list of causes. The procedures summarized below may be useful in helping the student teacher feel more comfortable with observers present:

Create an "open door" policy in your classroom or department
    Others come in to get materials, observe, or work
    Frequent visits of professional personnel in classrooms can make the situation seem less foreboding because it is more routine
Invite the student teacher to observe your work
    Encourage student teachers and other teachers to make suggestions which might improve your teaching style
Do something besides sit and look at the student teacher while in the room
    Quietly move around in the back, checking materials, setting up displays or checking references

Appear preoccupied by such activities as grading papers or leafing through some publication

Use discretion in writing

Make a practice of sharing written comments with the student teacher

Arrange to work with an individual or a small group of pupils while the student teacher is involved in teaching

Show positive reinforcement through smiles and other encouraging facial expressions

Observe frequently

Avoid interruptions in class

Make follow-up suggestions that emphasize the improvement of learning for the class instead of criticism of the student teacher's performance

Student teachers usually seem more apprehensive if they know in advance that an observation will occur. This is especially likely in connection with a visit from the university supervisor or by an administrator or department head. The unexpected, informal visit is likely to be less traumatic.

Case Study No. 41: A SUPERVISING TEACHER FAILS TO OBSERVE FOR SEVERAL DAYS

You are convinced that you are indeed fortunate to have such a competent student teacher. He is energetic, pleasant, and knowledgeable. After several weeks of student teaching, he has met every task to your satisfaction. Since he has been doing well, you have taken the opportunity to catch up on some work and have not observed his teaching for two weeks. Now you begin to wonder if you should visit the class more frequently. When you mention this to your student teacher, he seems mildly surprised and his response is that he feels that he is progressing satisfactorily and does not need help. How do you respond to him?

1. Suggest that since he is doing well you might be able to help him initiate more sophisticated teaching techniques
2. Indicate that you have left him alone because you have been busy
3. Mention that you must soon write the final evaluation and that you want to have evidence of his more recent performances for that evaluation
4. Stress that you are interested in learning some ideas from him
5. State that it is always a good idea to have another professional study a teacher's work regardless of his level of performance

6. Suggest that he observe some of your teaching and comment on it _____
7. _____

Consider:

a. Implications of the practice of not observing the
   student teacher for an extended period of time
b. Teaching skills that can be developed after initial
   adjustments have been made
c. Development of a positive attitude toward supervised
   observations
d. _____

INTERRUPTING THE STUDENT TEACHER: **The Alarm Goes Off**

The design of a student teaching program unavoidably creates a
degree of anxiety. A teaching candidate is being scrutinized by an individual who has been recognized for teaching competence, and his
future may rest upon the judgment of this experienced teacher. The
student teacher is in the process of realizing that he does not know
everything about subject matter, classroom management, student
behavior or teaching technique. His demeanor with the class may be
precarious and any move by the teacher which is perceived by the
student teacher as a criticism or an attempt to help with an inadequacy
may be disconcerting to him if it is made in the presence of a group of
pupils.

The supervising teacher is concerned with the progress of the class
as well as the growth of the student teacher. His breaking into the
class routine may be natural to him and his comments may be intended
for the overall good of both pupils and student teacher. He may not read
the feelings of his subordinate or comprehend the possible change of
attitude the class might direct toward the student teacher.

A teacher is most likely to be tempted to interrupt in a class
whenever:

A student teacher makes an error in subject matter
The supervising teacher wishes to provide supplementary knowledge or
   an illustration
The supervising teacher feels that a pupil should be corrected or
   disciplined
The student teacher gets into a difficulty and does not know how to
   correct it

Interventions by a supervising teacher are usually disconcerting experiences for a student teacher. Regardless of the teacher's good intentions, the student teacher may perceive that he has been exposed to the
class as unable to perform the task at hand. It may be difficult for him to
regain his composure or confidence.

The supervising teacher's unilateral injection into the class discussion may correct an immediate difficulty, but it can initiate a more serious problem. Such an intervention can produce a lack of confidence on the part of the student teacher and a lack of pupil respect for him. It can convey the idea that the student teacher is actually a puppet responding to the directions of his master. Interruptions should occur only when irreversible damage is being done to the class.

A good planning conference between the supervising teacher and student teacher should alert both parties to any potential problems and they can discuss methods of avoiding them if they do occur. Most other concerns can be discussed after class and then the student teacher can make the necessary adjustments in an ensuing session. A mistake in content, for example, can be explained by the student teacher the following day with no real problems as far as the pupils are concerned.

Case Study No. 42: THE STUDENT TEACHER RUNS OUT OF MATERIAL AND THE SUPERVISING TEACHER IS TEMPTED TO INTERRUPT TO HELP HIM

The student teacher is teaching one of his more complicated lessons and you are observing from the rear of the room. Although he has done a lot of study and preparation, he fails to develop many points in the presentation and hurries from topic to topic. His planned forty-minute lesson is completed in half that time. He has nothing else to say and you know that the study period will not keep students occupied the remainder of the time. He finishes his exercise and looks at you. What do you do?

1. Say nothing and let him experience the long period of time with no planned activity
2. Take over the class and provide additional explanation of material which has just been covered
3. Take over the class and engage them in conversation concerning another topic or idea
4. After the pupils have obviously finished their study, start a discussion of some type which will utilize the remaining time.
5. Say nothing, but demand that the pupils follow the student teacher's instructions in the event that confusion occurs.
6: _____

Consider:

a. More thorough analysis of plans, particularly in regard to insuring that the student teacher understands procedures for adequately developing a lesson
b. A discussion of procedures whereby lessons can be extended (review, summaries, etc.)
c. Potential techniques for cooperative arrangements in case a plan fails
d. _____

Case Study No. 43: THE STUDENT TEACHER PRESENTS IN-FORMATION WHICH CONTRADICTS WHAT THE SUPER-VISING TEACHER HAD ALREADY TAUGHT

The content of some topics can be approached by more than one method. All are correct, but continuity is important if the pupils are not to be confused. The impact of this is made apparent to you one day when the student teacher is making a demonstration and suggests steps which are contrary to those you have already taught and which will cause the students to be confused by his technique. As the student teacher explains his system, several puzzled pupils look your way knowing that you had given them different instructions. What do you do?

1. Interrupt and explain that each method is satisfactory, but that they should follow your plan since it has already been inaugurated
2. Remain silent and see what happens, hoping that the student teacher will notice and make the correction or ask you to comment
3. Discuss the problem after class and suggest a method of reconciling the differences in technique
4. Permit the student teacher to proceed with his method
5. _____

Consider:

a. Implications of adapting to another system
b. Techniques of reconciling the differences and still maintaining class respect for the student teacher
c. Overall emotional climate between student teacher, supervising teacher, and class
d. Preventive communication
e. _____

Case Study No. 44: THE STUDENT TEACHER COMMUNICATES AN SOS

In a lively discussion the student teacher successfully arouses the interest of the pupils. Several penetrating questions were correctly answered by the student teacher. Then one of the more intelligent pupils in class asks a searching question that the student teacher cannot answer. She mumbles a bit, rephrases the question, and desperately looks at you. What do you do?

1. Answer the question for the pupil
2. Avoid looking at the student teacher and let her resolve the matter in her own way
3. Break in under some pretense and then respond to the question, providing cues for the student teacher so that she can make the final point
4. _____

Consider:

a. The effect upon the student teacher if she is left unable to answer a question
b. A method by which answers can be interjected without the appearance of taking over from the student teacher
c. A discussion of alternatives in accepting questions which a teacher cannot answer
d. ————————————————————

Case Study No. 45: THE TEMPTATION TO CORRECT AN OBVIOUS ERROR

You are observing your student teacher when he commits a rather serious error of knowledge as he talks with the class. The student teacher gives no indication that he recognizes that the error has been committed and the pupils will assume that it is true unless it is corrected. If they are not informed, serious difficulty could occur later as they do the homework which will be assigned. What course of action do you take?

1. Intervene and make the necessary correction
2. Attempt to subtly get the student teacher's attention and then have him recognize you for comment
3. Remain silent, but discuss the error with him at the first opportunity so that he can make the necessary correction
4. If he provides time for study, talk with him and then he can explain the error to the class after you leave the room
5. ————————————————————

Consider:

a. The effect of interruption on the student teacher's confidence and on the pupils' perceptions of him
b. The actual implications of the erroneous information
c. Possible arrangements for unobvious communication with the student teacher
d. ————————————————————

SUPERVISION BY COOPERATIVE TEACHING: **Working Together in the Fish Bowl**

Cooperative teaching can be a valuable part of a student teaching experience throughout the entire period as well as during the initial days. The cooperative, or team, arrangement is a dimension of professional activity which has the potential for enriching teaching skills. Professional educators can learn from each other as they work together on a mutual task. Team teaching provides an avenue in which the particular skills of each teacher may be utilized more effectively. The cooperative plan creates an opportunity for more creative activities as teachers working together pool their knowledge, ideas, and skills.

A cooperative arrangement has long been accepted as a procedure for induction into a profession or trade. The combination of mutual goals, shared responsibility, and contact with more experienced and more knowledgeable persons creates a climate for learning. Conversely, newer learnings of the inductee can be shared with the experienced practitioner. The team situation provides an easier method for an individual to assume important responsibility gradually instead of having it suddenly thrust upon him. In the field of education, cooperation in the more complex teaching situations is particularly desirable.

Role definition is important in this type of arrangement. Functions must be clearly understood by each party, and each participant should know his own sphere of operation. In addition, each participant must perceive his role as important to the accomplishment of the team task.

This team approach is especially recommended when the class can logically be grouped or taught in a cooperative arrangement. Reading groups, physical education classes, and laboratory groups all provide opportunities for such an approach. This method has the built-in advantage of providing the opportunity for a supervising teacher to assist a student teacher who may be having problems without the pupils perceiving that difficulties exist.

The responsibility of the student teacher for the activities he is directing should be apparent to him. This delegated responsibility in cooperative teaching insures an independence of action on his part since he can feel that he is not just following the directions of the supervising teacher. It further implies that he is accountable for his actions and decisions.

Case Study No. 46: PUPILS TURN TO THE SUPERVISING TEACHER FOR ASSISTANCE INSTEAD OF SEEKING OUT THE STUDENT TEACHER

Your student teacher has assigned an activity project and you are in the room to see that it develops satisfactorily. Since the pupils are accustomed to working with you, they begin to come to you with their questions instead of asking the student teacher. Before long, you find that four to five students may be waiting to ask for your assistance while the student teacher has no one waiting to seek his help. What should you do?

1. Continue to help the pupils assuming that those waiting will go to the student teacher eventually
2. Tell the pupils that Mr. ———————— is the teacher for this project and that he should be asked
3. Quickly leave the room

4. Announce to the class that both of you can give assistance if needed, but if one is busy, the pupil should go to the other teacher
5. —————————————————————————————

Consider:

a. The effect that your assistance will have upon the confidence of the student teacher
b. The effect that your lack of participation will have on the pupils
c. Pre-planning of project activities so that questions are at a minimum
d. Possible effective utilization of both student teacher and supervising teacher
e. —————————————————————————

Case Study No. 47: THE STUDENT TEACHER RESISTS WORKING WITH DIFFICULT GROUPS

In your highly-structured activity class, you have the pupils divided into ability groups, and you have been rotating with the student teacher so that she can work with the different levels of students. After a while she begins to seek means of avoiding working with the "problem section." Finally, she comments that she would like to work with Group One all the time because she does not ever intend to teach slow students. She further states that she feels she is not able to accomplish anything with the slow learners. What is your response?

1. Grant her request and let her work with the group she chooses
2. Explain that she should be prepared for all levels of teaching regardless of her present intentions
3. Point out that teaching techniques used with slower students may be just as beneficial in work with brighter ones, and that since one has to work harder with the more reluctant learners, he may learn better how to teach the more advanced pupils
4. Discuss techniques which will help her to be more effective with the problem group
5. —————————————————————————

Consider:

a. Background information about each section
b. The real learning value of difficult classes
c. The value of a comprehensive look at teaching
d. The explanation of the responsibility delegated
e. The effect of failure on attitude and future plans
f. —————————————————————

Case Study No. 48: THE SUPERVISING TEACHER HAS DIF-FICULTY DELEGATING RESPONSIBILITY TO HIS STUDENT TEACHER

Since teaching has been your life, you find that you can organize and perform its tasks efficiently and effectively. As a result, the cooperative work with your student teacher finds you assuming the major role, including organizing the class, getting equipment together, and directing learning activities. Almost without your realizing it, your student teacher becomes a subordinate, performing only the more menial tasks. In a conversation, she hints that she would like to take complete responsibility for the next unit. Since you have many good ideas for this unit already, what do you do?

1. Allow her to develop the unit as she wishes
2. Allow her to develop the unit, but show her what you have done previously
3. Suggest that she will learn more if you continue in your same role
4. _____

Consider:

a. The nature of real responsibility assumed by the student teacher
b. Procedures for delegating actual responsibility to the student teacher
c. The validity of the assumptions concerning the student teacher's capabilities

d. _____

THE STUDENT TEACHER'S RESPONSIBILITY FOR DISCIPLINE: **Who Keeps the Paddle?**

The nature of classroom discipline may be rather poorly conceptualized by the student teacher. His utterances may be piloted by feelings of insecurity which were initiated by the new challenges of adjusting to student teaching. He may feel at the beginning that the most important criterion in student teaching will be the ability to establish control over the class.

The greatest problem in maintaining discipline may be that the student teacher will adopt a behavior pattern which represents one of the polarized views about student control. On one hand he may literally accept the advice of the teacher who says that you start out tough and then relax as control is insured. At the other extreme, he may feel that he can best secure cooperation by being a nice person, indeed by proving to the students that he is really one of them. If the student teacher chooses either of these roles the nearly inevitable results are frustration for the student teacher and problems for the supervising teacher.

A supervising teacher must avoid being too protective, because the student teacher cannot learn classroom management if he is dependent on the strong personality of another teacher. Supervising teachers' comments to the class such as, "If you do not behave for the student teacher, you will answer to me," only confirm the suspicions of the class and the student teacher that this beginner really is not capable of establishing satisfactory relationships by himself.

One of the major skills which the student teacher must learn is to interact effectively with his class. The impact of his own personality has to be the determining variable in creating a successful classroom environment. He needs independence in order to succeed, but he also must have the assistance of one who has already solved the problem of creating effective relationships in a democratic manner. The student nearly always enters student teaching with discipline as his major worry, and his primary wish is that he will be able to survive in a classroom filled with pupils. The supervising teacher should begin immediately to help him develop a more comprehensive and positive approach in the area of classroom management.

The student teacher's authority will be derived from the supervising teacher who must determine the degree of responsibility which he may assume. An early conference to discuss the student teacher's role would be helpful to the anxious learner. At this time general guidelines could be agreed upon. This conference should normally cover the following areas:

Any policy which the school adheres to in regard to discipline in general and corporal punishment in particular

The nature of student behavior and how desired behavior can be achieved by positive means

The specific policies and procedures in the area of discipline which the supervising teacher believes and practices

The amount of authority or responsibility which the student teacher is expected to exercise

Any guidelines which the university provides, e.g., the prohibition by the administration of corporal punishment by a student teacher

Case Study No. 49: A CONFLICT WITH A PROBLEM PUPIL

You have left the student teacher alone with the class. At its conclusion he reports that he had a problem with Stan, who apparently refused to obey a command. He said first that he asked Stan in a nice way to comply with his order. When the boy initially refused, he demanded that he obey, but still the pupil would not cooperate. At that point your student teacher grabbed the argumentative pupil, shook him, and told him to obey immediately. Stan argued and several other pupils began to jeer. Since the supervising teacher was not available, he took the boy directly to the dean, and the bell sounded before he returned to class. He will have to face the class tomorrow, and Stan will probably be back. What should you do to prepare the student teacher for the next encounter with the class?

1. Remain away again and let the student teacher work out the problem
2. Be in the class the next day, but remain silent unless some incident occurs
3. Take charge of the class the next day and reprimand the students for their behavior
4. Plan some disciplinary measures that the student teacher can administer and let him follow through
5. Plan some procedures with the student teacher so that he can have a good chance of solving any problem that might occur the next day
6. Discuss various alternatives of handling problem situations which might not get the student teacher so involved in a defensive stance
7. ———————————————————————

   Consider:

   a. Proper interpretation of school policy in regard to discipline
   b. The importance of having knowledge about students
   c. Emergency procedures which the student teacher can employ
   d. Discussion of alternative procedures for reacting to hostility
   e. ———————————————————

Case Study No. 50: A PUPIL THREATENS THE STUDENT TEACHER

As part of providing a total experience for your student teacher, you have asked her to supervise your study hall. One day when you were not present, she asked a pupil to sit down and he refused to comply. The student teacher then indicated that if he did not take his seat, he would be referred to the dean. The pupil, who happens to be on probation, reponded with a threat of an "accident" after school. The student teacher, although frightened, sent a referral note to the dean. She described the incident to you and expressed the fear that the pupil might actually try some type of retribution. She indicated that this incident unnerved her and asked to be relieved of the study hall responsibilities. What course of action do you pursue?

1. Remove the student teacher from further contacts with the study hall

2. Insist that she return the next day and appear to be poised
3. Return to the study hall with the student teacher the next day
4. Discuss alternative procedures in managing tense situations
5. Report the incident and the threat to the proper personnel
6. Suggest that the student teacher arrange a private conversation with the pupil and attempt to appeal to reasonable actions
7. See that the student teacher's personal safety is assured
8. _____

Consider:

a. The context that may have prompted the remark by the pupil
b. Discussion of procedures of study hall management
c. Discussion of alternative procedures of securing student cooperation
d. _____

Case Study No. 51: THE STUDENT TEACHER QUESTIONS THE SCHOOL'S DISCIPLINARY ACTION TAKEN AGAINST ONE OF HER PUPILS

Kim is idealistic. She believes that it is more important to try to prevent problems than it is to punish students for misbehavior. She was assigned a class of remedial students and she worked hard to teach them while concurrently attempting to help them evolve into better citizens. She had managed to make some progress with Harvey, one of the most uncooperative students in the group. She was pleased with the stated policy that the school recognized that pupils should be kept in school if possible and that instruction should be adjusted to the student's level.

Her idealism was shaken when she learned that Harvey had been expelled by the dean for smoking in the rest room. He would lose credit for the entire semester's work in spite of the fact that there were only nine days remaining. She questioned you about the school's conflicting policy of trying to "save pupils" on one hand and yet being so arbitrary about a smoking rule. She pointed out that teachers smoke all the time in the lounge and no one takes any action against them. She asks for your permission to express her thoughts to the administrator who expelled Harvey. What do you do?

1. Arrange for an appointment with the dean
2. Dismiss the incident, making certain to specify that the pupil was aware of the rule against smoking
3. Suggest that her teaching was not in vain because he obviously learned something while he was in the class
4. Petition for the boy's reinstatement, supporting it by the progress he has recently made in class
5. _____

Consider:

a. The context of school rules
b. The effect upon the student teacher's interest and enthusiasm
c. Implications of the decision upon the pupil
d. ─────────────────────────────

ANALYZING TEACHING: **What It's All About**

The contemporary thought in professional education points out that teaching is behavior which can be described and modified. The behavioral characteristics have been identified in various research studies during the past few years or justified by theoretical constructs. The categories can be subsumed into two major areas: (1) intellectual manipulation of subject matter, and (2) personal relationships between the teacher and students.

A commission report by the Association for Student Teaching[1] on the study of teaching states:

"Student teaching in teacher education should offer opportunities for self-appraisal of the appropriateness of various styles of teaching for accomplishing specified objectives. Student teaching should be thought of as a time to study teaching as well as practice teaching. It is a time to put untried ideas to the test in a variety of real situations, and to study the results.

"The study of teaching requires specialized skills. Prospective teachers can learn these skills, and supervisors can be trained to help preservice and inservice teachers to analyze behavior.

"Teacher education, therefore, should include experiences which prepare preservice and inservice teachers in the study and practice of teaching, as well as experiences which prepare supervisors in the study and practice of supervision."

The supervising teacher should concentrate on those factors in teaching which are recognized as valid skills. The professional experience offers the best opportunity for the student teacher to identify those behaviors and incorporate them into his own style of teaching. Many different descriptions exist, but the following criteria were carefully researched and developed in a federal research project concerned with determining factors related to success in student teaching.[2] This profile represents the positive teaching behaviors that were identified in that endeavor:

1 Commission on the Implications of Recent Research in Teaching, **The Study of Teaching,** Association for Student Teaching, 1967, preface.

2 Donald M. Sharpe, **Isolating Relevant Variables in Student Teacher Assessment,** U. S. Office of Education, 1969, Contract No. OEC-3-7-061321-0342.

Understanding, friendly
>   Friendly, understanding, tactful, good natured
>   Shows concern for a pupil's personal needs
>   Tolerant of errors on the part of pupils
>   Finds good things in pupils and calls attention to them
>   Listens encouragingly to pupil's viewpoints

Planned and organized
>   Businesslike, systematic, consistent, thorough, well-prepared
>   Has a detailed lesson plan or other evidence of thorough planning
>   Plans ahead
>   Objectives are clearly discernible
>   Tells class what to expect during the period
>   Has needed materials ready
>   Keeps good records

Stimulating and imaginative
>   Original, encourages pupil initiative
>   Interesting presentation--holds student interest
>   Animated, enthusiastic
>   Capitalizes on student interest

Possesses self-confidence
>   Sees self as liked, worthy, and able to do a good job
>   Speaks confidently; confident in relations with students
>   Poised
>   Takes mistakes and criticisms in stride
>   Accepts new tasks readily

Mastery of subject matter
>   Recognizes important and significant knowledge in his field--concepts; generalizations
>   Focuses class presentations on these basic concepts
>   Relates to other fields or traces implications for the knowledge

Communicates well and emphathetically
>   Shows acute sensitivity to the perceptions of pupils
>   Makes presentations at students' level of understanding
>   Draws examples from local community or current interests of age group being taught
>   Makes effective use of media
>   Has no distracting mannerisms
>   Speaks well

Classroom discourse characterized by reasoning and creative thinking
>   Helps students go beyond specific recall of facts into an understanding and application of problem solving
>   Seeks definition of problems in class and leads the pupils to consider solutions
>   Asks open-ended questions (frequently asks "why")
>   Encourages application of knowledge

Encourages students to see the relationship of facts to each other

Directs attention to the logical operations in teaching

Seeks definition of terms

Points out differences between what is observed and what is inferred from the observation

Demands examination of evidence

Leads students to state assumptions

Examines beliefs and opinions

The student teacher will have a valuable experience if he goes no further than being able to recognize his capacity in performing the above skills and understanding their impact. The supervising teacher can most effectively stress the importance of the preceding skills by demonstrating them in his own teaching. He will then be in a better position to help the student teacher evaluate himself and assist in the development of more sophisticated teaching behavior. Lastly, it should become apparent that certain teaching moves can bring about predictable results.

Worksheet No. 5: AN ACTIVITY PROFILE FOR USE IN STUDENT TEACHER ANALYSIS

Observation of teaching can be of more value to the student teacher if the experience can be reconstructed, the effectiveness of the teaching acts discussed, and alternatives considered. The **Teacher Classroom Activity Profile**[3] is one form which can provide a sequential account of the major activities in which the student teacher engages during the class session:

TEACHER ACTIVITY		3 MINUTE INTERVALS																								SUMMARY	
		1	2	3	4	5	6	7	8	9	10	11	12	13	14	15	16	17	18	19	20	21	22	23	24	MINUTES	PER CENT
NAGEMENT−NON−LEARNING	MN																											
NAGEMENT−LEARNING	ML																											
SENTATION	P																											
ITATION	R																											
CUSSION	D																											
ICAL THINKING	L.T.																											
NKING PROCESS	T.P																											

EXPLANATORY NOTES: ANECDOTAL NOTES:

DATE _____ SIGNED _____

---

3 **Ibid.**

Definition of Major Categories of TCAP

MN - Management (Non-learning)
Management of classroom when the teacher is not attempting to teach, e.g., reading announcements, taking roll, distributing materials, organizing equipment, idle time, disciplining pupils, waiting for bell to ring.

ML - Management (Learning)
Management of classroom so that learning may occur but the teacher is not involved except in a managerial role, e.g., showing a sound film, administering a written examination, supervising study time, student reports

Presentation
The presentation of subject matter by the teacher in some organized fashion, e.g., lectures, demonstrations, illustrated talks, blackboard presentation, reading

Recitation/Drill
The solicitation of student responses which call for terse memorized data, oral testing to determine if assignments have been read, review questions, drill, and practice time

Discussion/Random
Random discussion involving student-teacher interaction but without analysis or synthesis. "Stream-of-consciousness" discussion without any apparent focus or purpose except to consume time until the period is over, e.g., "Talk-talk-talk"

LT - Logical Thinking
Discussion which involves analysis and synthesis. The teacher is deliberately encouraging or permitting thinking to occur. This category is more than reciting or repeating something which has been learned or memorized

Thinking Process
Deliberate, conscious attention on the part of the teacher to the intellectual process, e.g., point out to the students the factual and/or logical basis of their thinking, pointing out errors in reasoning, examining the reliability and validity of evidence, defining terms, checking assumptions, examining the scientific method, examining values, seeking reason for conflicting opinions, examining the method of inquiry

The observer records a continuous line moving among the seven activities in three-minute intervals. If there is just a momentary shift in categories, a vertical line going up or down to the proper category should be made without interruption of the general flow of the regular profile graphs. It has been found helpful to indicate the time at the top of the three-minute interval columns, starting in column 1 with the minute

TEACHER CLASSROOM ACTIVITY PROFILE

STUDENT TEACHER ___Kay Smith___ ———— Date ————

CLASS ___Home Economics-Junior High___ TYPE ———— SUPERVISOR ___Scott___

Teacher Activity	Intel. Level	9:00 1	9:03 2	9:06 3	9:09 4	9:12 5	9:15 6	9:18 7	9:21 8	9:24 9	9:27 10	9:30 11	9:33 12	9:36 13	9:39 14	9:42 15	9:45 16	9:48 17	9:51 18	9:54 19	9:57 20	Approx. Min.	Approx. %
MN Management—Non-Learning	1																					1	2
ML Management—Learning	1																					24	40
P Presentation	2																					20	33
R Recitation/Drill	2																					0	0
D Random Discussion	2																					5	8
LT Logical Thinking	3																					9	15
TP Thinking Process	4																					1	2

3 Minute Intervals / Summary

Explanatory Notes

1. Quiz
6. Distribute duplicated materials - Students read
8. Filmstrip "Book Before" - Teacher interjects comments
14. Question: "What do you think the purpose of the film was?"
15. Write down your meaning of nutrition
15. Students offer definition of nutrition
16. Instruction: "Write down what you ate yesterday"
17. Discussion of what was eaten yesterday
18. Question: "Do we really eat well?"
19. Pupils arrive at a definition of nutrients
20. Teacher presents a list of terms

Anecdotal Records

1. Do you think that an introduction to the filmstrip would have been of value?
2. Coordination of filmstrip and sound was excellent
3. Are there any ideas that should be summarized from the questions concerning the value of the film?
4. Are there any conclusions concerning the food consumed yesterday?
5. Good question - pursue it further
6. The end of class did not seem to be a good time to introduce terms? Could it wait until the next class session?
7. Several different techniques were used. Students maintained interest.
8. Students were thinking. Continue to get them involved
9. Circle arrangement of class seemed to create a good atmosphere for discussion

the class starts and then recording the time at three-minute intervals after that in the numbered squares. Explanatory notes are keyed to the column number which indicates the sequence of three-minute intervals. Evaluative comments are recorded in the section designated as "Anecdotal Records."

The example on page 105 illustrates a completed form.

The Teacher Classroom Activity Profile:

Describes

the way a teacher spends time in the classroom

the type of intellectual activity utilized

the number of activities utilized

Gives clues to

whether objectives are being met

organizational patterns

possible teaching problems

Enables a teacher

to reconstruct his own experience for examination

to formulate conclusions toward his success in teaching

SUPERVISING PARTICIPATION IN PUPIL EVALUATION: The Curve Becomes a Question Mark

One of the most exciting activities for the student teacher is participation in the evaluation of pupil achievement. If the student teacher is allowed to share in this process, he will feel that he has earned his teacher's confidence in his ability to make valid appraisals. A student teacher's self-confidence can be quickly shattered, though, as he begins to wrestle with the dilemma of grading. The first test results can be more effective in criticizing a student teacher than all the exhortations a supervisor can employ. If he has covered the material too rapidly or too abstractly, he will be informed by low test results. If he finds that the grades are too high, he will learn that he has made the test too easy or has been teaching below the pupils' potential. He may discover that the terminology or phrasing of a test was so obscure that the results cannot be considered valid.

The evaluation procedure provides a situation where a student teacher may gain a more valid concept of pupil ability. The boy who had all the answers in class may have produced a rather unimpressive test response, and the girl whose name he could not recall may have received the highest score in the group. Other visible cues of writing and expression may present an understanding of pupils which so far had evaded the student teacher.

The beginning student teacher is apt to possess a very limited concept of evaluation. In his thinking, a test may be the objective for teaching, and quizzes are punitive devices designed to force students to complete assignments. Comments such as, "Read the chapter; we may have a test on it tomorrow," may permeate his assignment procedures. A pupil may be referred to as an "A" or "D" student as if that designation presents an accurate and comprehensive profile of a child. This is particularly true when it can be reinforced by quoting an IQ test score. Even more significant may be the fact that the student teacher sees evaluation as an end instead of a process for analysis of instruction. Evaluation may be determined by some poorly worded specific-recall questions instead of a more sophisticated examination, and there may be a propensity to fail to consider factors in evaluation other than test results.

The origin of this superficial concept may have arisen from a lack of experience and a lack of example. It is possible that, as a college student with limited experience, he failed to prepare for the ultimate necessity of evaluation. The student teacher will undoubtedly have a great amount of insight to gain and possible attitudes to alter in regard to evaluation. The supervising teacher can take nothing for granted here.

The joint approach to evaluation is usually preferable. This process enables the supervisor to be in a better position to help the student teacher develop a more adequate concept of how to make a valid appraisal of progress. The objectives of this shared approach should lead to a student teacher's formulation of a more comprehensive outlook in regard to evaluation. Consider the following as desirable goals to be achieved by the joint approach:

It should help the student teacher understand the role of pupil evaluation
    A tool for growth instead of an instrument for judgment
    Pupil evaluation reports serve as guides in future teaching of the class
It should help the student teacher understand the total process of evaluation
    Various techniques of evaluation
    Different types of examinations and quizzes
    Methods in determining letter grades
It should help the student teacher understand what a student is capable of achieving
    A college student's recent association with his peers may have caused him to forget that many pupils learn slowly
It should ensure that the student teacher understands the criteria which can be considered in determining a grade

After the student teacher gains some understanding of the evaluation process, he should apply his knowledge through participation in the determination of grades. The supervising teacher will want to review and approve the assigned grades with the student teacher before they are announced to the pupils since final responsibility cannot be delegated to another. The student teacher can gain a lot of confidence if he discovers that his evaluation roughly corresponds to that of the supervising teacher.

Case Study No. 52: THE FIRST TEST RESULTS PROVE TO BE DISCOURAGING

Your student teacher had worked hard in the preparation of his first test and had been anticipating reviewing its results as a means of determining his effectiveness as a teacher. It was carefully explained and closely supervised, but the results were disastrous. There were two "C's," three "D's," and nineteen "F's" in a class that was considered average or slightly above average.

As a teacher of the class and as a supervisor of the student teacher, you:

1. Let the results stand
2. Do not count the results of the test and so inform the class
3. Do not count the test results, but do not inform the class
4. Suggest that the student teacher revise his grading scale to make it more consistent with prior test results
5. Suggest that he administer another test and count only the higher test score for the purposes of evaluation
6. _____

Consider:

a. Review of a test before its administration
b. Discussion of standards in evaluation
c. The necessity of your review and approval before test results are announced
d. _____

WRITTEN COMMUNICATION IN SUPERVISION: **The Positive Values of Writer's Cramp**

Communication is a problem and a necessity in nearly any human situation. The student teaching environment presents situations which can make it even more difficult. Since accurate exchanges of ideas are imperative to a good student teaching program, every possible procedure has to be utilized in order to maintain understanding and to increase information sharing. A lack of spoken or written conversation can create confusion and nurture an environment where erroneous assumptions can flourish. Written comments can help prevent a real gap in communication and comprehension.

A principal purpose of written communication is to encourage student teachers and cooperating teachers to think about student teaching. This interplay of ideas becomes a dialogue which serves as a record of past performance and a resource file of suggestions which could be applicable in future teaching. It is believed that a student teacher best develops by consciously formulating and examining hypotheses in the light of his experience. He should state such hypotheses from time to time and record evidence which bears upon the case. By sharing in this process, the cooperating teacher makes a valuable contribution to the professional growth of the teaching candidate.

Comments by both supervising teacher and student teacher which are made in writing provide an additional opportunity to share thoughts and ideas. Writing offers a method of exchanging views and information in student teaching when conversation is not possible. A teacher observing his student may want to communicate several ideas as he views his work. Since conversation is impossible at this point and since one may forget many thoughts if he does not make note of them, writing becomes a valuable procedure. Written comments can be useful in developing clarity of thinking, too, in that it gives both teacher and student teacher an opportunity to consider precisely what is to be said.

Some universities require their student teachers to keep a journal, or log, which is designated for such interaction. This running commentary, used properly, has the advantage of describing the continuous progress of the student teacher.

In summary, written communication can achieve the following functions:

Evaluates the progress of the student teacher
 Provides immediate reaction to the teaching situation
 Offers suggestions for improvements
 Indicates what and why a lesson was well taught
 Provides encouragement for the student teacher to record self-evaluative comments for the teacher's reaction
Makes a permanent record of useful teaching ideas
 How to manage certain situations in teaching
 How to cope with designated problems which generally arise in working with pupils
 Ideas for such procedures as introducing a lesson and interjecting variety into a classroom routine
 Sources of instructional materials and aids
Determines contractual arrangements
 Defines responsibilities
 Clarifies verbal agreements
Encourages reflection
 Helps the student teacher to think about his work

> Examines ideas and practices

Provides a record of professional information about students and the school

> School procedures and regulations
> Semi-confidential information about students

Written comments which are made on a regular basis can create better communication with a student teacher. He can soon see the value of having so many of the important aspects of student teaching recorded for further reference.

Worksheet No. 6: A FORM FOR WRITTEN COMMUNICATION

A stenographer's notebook provides an excellent form for written communication. It is economical, durable, easy to use, and the middle line provides a natural divider which allows the responses to flow naturally.

Writing is especially effective when conversation is not possible and when more significant observations are made and should be remembered. The following illustrations demonstrate the type of communication that is typically recorded, although the nature of the responses are limited only by the creativity of the writers. Remember, the student teacher will place greater significance upon those comments which are recorded.

Student-Teacher	Supervising Teacher
Perhaps that is why I received little response. I will work on that.	It is difficult to respond to a question like "How about maps?" because the query has no specific direction to it.
What did you think of the class today?	You did this well. Had attention of students Film introduction told them what to look for Related the ideas to present experience Instructions on notes were vague Be prepared for that extra five minutes of time--Review, perhaps
Thank you	
How would you start a class in shorthand at the beginning of the year?	On the first day I ask them to copy down what I read. I then read at 90 WPM and they are all lost in a minute or two. I then explain that shorthand will enable them to record words that fast by the end of the year.

Student Teacher	**Supervising Teacher**
I will have it ready by then	Let's try to get the bulletin board display ready by Monday
Gary is a very poor student and consumes so much time. I wonder if it is fair for the others for him to be in school at all.	He may be a lot of trouble and a slow learner, but we hope he is at least developing some attitudes and values which will make him a better person. I am convinced that we would be in a worse condition if we ignored the Gary's in our world. A doctor spends more time with his sick patients; a teacher also has to devote more time for his "sick" students.
I will try that tomorrow.	You are not getting much student interaction. You might arrange the chairs in a circle to see if you get more student-to-student responses.
I did not know what to do with Joe today, when he started acting cute.	Joe suffers from lack of attention. Check his personal file and then let's talk about some ways of reaching him.
I will think about that.	Except for your family, the most important factor in your life will be that of striving to be an excellent teacher. Such times as washing dishes, dusting the house, or walking to school can provide moments for reflection and planning for teaching. You must live, eat, and sleep good teaching. It must become your life.

Case Study No. 53: THE STUDENT TEACHER WHO IS RELUCTANT TO WRITE

As a supervising teacher you feel that systematic written communication is essential, but your student teacher hesitates to put anything down on paper. He constantly "forgets" his journal and does not respond to your written comments. Since you feel that such communication is necessary, what do you do?

1. Inform him that the journal is to be in the room at all times and that you expect him to make certain entries in it
2. Continue writing, although he does not give any indication of having read your comments

3. Discontinue writing in obvious deference to his implied wishes
4. Discuss the situation with the student teacher and try to determine why he feels that such communication is not important
5. Inform the college supervisor of his lack of cooperation
6. _____

Consider:

a. The purposes of written communication
b. The techniques of making written comments less threatening to the student teacher
c. The overall relationship that exists between the two of you in regard to evaluative consideration
d. _____

Brian was about fifteen minutes into his lesson when Miss Bennett returned to the room. As he continued teaching, she cast a few knowing glances as he successfully maneuvered through a few potentially difficult explanations. After a while she reached for the journal and entered a few comments. When class was finished, they discussed the development of the lesson. Miss Bennett began by inquiring about the introduction and then asked for Brian's reaction to the lesson. After his comments, she added, "I think that you showed considerable improvement in your development of thinking today. The questions caused the pupils to relate the material we have been working with for the last week. I think they will be more sophisticated in their future work because of this series of lessons."

Brian agreed and then glanced at the journal. Miss Bennett caught the cue and handed the book to him. "I wrote down a thought or two about your teaching style in general as you had requested. A little attention to the details which I have mentioned can help you with a few of your concerns. I also wrote down some ideas for teaching the next unit which you might like to consider in your preparation."

While Brian was reading the comments, Miss Bennett continued organizing some materials which Brian had started and which were to be used for the group which was due in the classroom in a few minutes. During this time, Joe Hanley walked by, looked in the room, formed a momentary puzzled look on his face, shrugged his shoulders, and sauntered on toward the teachers' lounge.

Remember:

Even when a supervising teacher does not wish it to be so, the student teacher will imitate many of the methods and practices of the supervising teacher

A supervising teacher has the duty to teach the student teacher how to teach

A group of student teachers were asked to offer suggestions concerning the supervisory techniques of their teachers. The following recommendations offer a great deal of insight into the principles that should guide a supervising teacher:

Do not turn the class over to the student teacher and leave - he will often need your assistance

Do not correct a student instead of letting the student teacher do it - this practice tends to make him feel inadequate

Do not interrupt the class while the student teacher is teaching

Be continuously aware of what the student teacher is doing

Be specific when you confer with the student teacher

USEFUL REFERENCES

ASSOCIATION FOR STUDENT TEACHING, *The Study of Teaching,* Commission on the Implications of Recent Research on Teaching, Association for Student Teaching, 1967, 91 pp.
Impact of recent research on teaching
Context for the study of teaching
Action programs

ASSOCIATION FOR STUDENT TEACHING, *Guiding Student Teaching Experiences,* Association for Student Teaching Bulletin No. 1, 1968
Supervisory guidelines

ASSOCIATION FOR STUDENT TEACHING, *The Student Teacher and Team Teaching,* Association for Student Teaching Bulletin No. 25, 1966
Team teaching

BROWN, CHARLES I., "Make it a Team Teaching Venture," *The Clearing House* 37:340-342, February, 1963
Team teaching

BROWN, THOMAS J., *Guiding A Student Teacher,* Harper, 1960, pp. 17-25
Cooperative teaching
Presentation of intellectual content

BRUBAKER, DALE, *The Teacher as a Decision-Maker,* William C. Brown Company, Dubuque, Iowa, 1970, Chapter 7
Sources of conflict between teachers and students

CURTIS, DWIGHT, AND ANDREWS, L. O., *Guiding Your Student Teacher,* Prentice-Hall, 1954, Chapter 9
Directing learning
Questions to stimulate learning
Evaluation of pupil growth
Interrruption by the teacher
Absence of the teacher from the class

DRAYER, ADAM, *Problems and Methods in High School Teaching,* D.C. Heath and Company, 1963, Chapter 5
Evaluation

FULLERTON, BILL, AND GRIFFITH, LeROY, *The Student Teacher and Team Teaching,* Association for Student Teaching Bulletin No. 25, 1966, 61 pp.
Cooperative teaching

GAMBONE, KENNETH, "Write to Your Student Teacher," *Journal of Teacher Education* 14:61-63, March, 1963
Written communication

GEGA, PETER C., AND BAKER, DOUGLAS, "A Log for Student Teaching Experiences," *The Journal of Teacher Education* 12:174-180, June, 1962
Written communication

HARRIS, BEN M., *Supervisory Behavior in Education,* Prentice-Hall, 1963, Chapter 5
Observations, analysis, and supervisory planning

HORTON, LOWELL, "Strikes, Sanctions, and the Student Teacher," *Contemporary Education* 43:1, October, 1971, pp. 38-39
  Guidelines for policy formulation of the role of the student teacher in strikes and sanctions
JENKINS, ORVILLE, "Team Teaching and the Intern," *Ohio School* 44:17, 31-32, January, 1966
  Team teaching
JONES, FRANKLIN B., *Legal Aspects of Student Teaching in the United States,* Unpublished doctoral dissertation, University of Mississippi, 1967
  Legal aspects
JORDAN, ARCHIE C., "Nine Steps to Improve the Classroom Experience of Student Teachers," *The Clearing House* 31:39-41, 1956
KIRK, JEFFREY, AND AMIDON, EDMUND, "When Student Teachers Study Interaction," *The Elementary School Journal* 68:79-104, November, 1967
LINDSEY, MARGARET, "The Teaching Team: Student Teacher and Supervising Teacher," *Teachers College Journal* 38:41-49, November, 1966.
LONGSTRETH, LARRY E., AND TAYLOR, BOB L., "Student Teaching-A Legal Vacuum," *Journal of Teacher Education* 22:1, Spring, 1971, pp 48-50
McGEOCH, DOROTHY, "Helping Student Teachers Become Students of Teaching," *Teachers College Journal* 39:18-21, October, 1967
  Analysis of teaching
O'HANLON, J. P., "Team Approach Provides Varied Student-Teaching Experience," *Minnesota Journal of Education* 43:12-14, November, 1967
  Cooperative teaching
O'CONNER, WILLIAM F., "Can Student Teachers Be Taught Classroom Control?" *Clearing House* 31:39-41, 1956
  Discipline
SHARPE, DONALD M., *Isolating Relevant Variables in Student Teacher Assessment,* U. S. Office of Education, 1969, Contract No. OEC-3-7-061321-0342
  Analyzing teaching
SHUMAN, BAIRD R., "Are Two Teachers in the Classroom Better Than One?" *Clearing House* 39:492-494, April, 1965
STRATEMEYER, FLORENCE, AND LINDSEY, MARGARET, *Working With Student Teachers,* Teachers College Press, 1958, Chapters 10, 11
  Guiding learning experiences
  Definitions of teaching
  Cooperative teaching
  Evaluation
SWALLS, FRED, *Legal Rights and Responsibilities of Indiana Teachers,* Interstate Printing and Publishing, Inc., Danville, Illinois, 1968, Chapter 7.
  Legal aspects
TANRUTHER, EDGAR, *Clinical Experiences in Teaching for the Student Teacher or Intern,* Dodd, Mead, and Company, 1967, Chapters 6, 8, 10
  Evaluation
  Discipline
  Analysis of teaching
TIESZEN, D. W., AND FOREMAN, CHARLES M., "Student Teaching--Some Legal Considerations," *The Journal of Teacher Education* 12:216-218, June, 1961
  Legal aspects
UNRUH, ADOLPH, AND TURNER, HAROLD E., *Supervision for Change and Innovation,* Houghton Mifflin Co., 1970, Chapter 2
  Communication and the effectiveness of supervision
WILES, KIMBALL, *Supervision for Better Schools,* Prentice-Hall, 1967, Chapter 5
  Application of communication theory to supervisory practices
WILSON, CHARLES F., "Student Teachers Adversely Affected by Super Supervision," *The Clearing House* 38:105-107, October, 1963
  Interrupting the student teacher

Chapter Eight

THE SUPERVISORY CONFERENCE

The university student teaching handbook suggested that a student teacher and his supervisor should conduct an extensive analysis of professional progress after a few weeks of student teaching. In accordance with this, Brian and Miss Bennett were discussing the details suggested in the handbook to see that all requirements were being met. Brian turned the page and said, "Look at this!" He began to read aloud.

Conferences are as essential to the student teaching experience as teaching if real professional growth is to be accomplished. This dialogue is a necessary procedure in providing complete analysis of the complex nature of teaching. A conference can help the student teacher solve immediate and long-range problems through the verbal input of his supervising teacher. Such conferences should be regular experiences for the teaching candidate."

Miss Bennett seemed mildly concerned. "Since you have been doing well, it has not seemed necessary to spend so much time in formal conferences. Do you think we should spend more time with such activity?". . .

THE CONFERENCE: **A Professional Mirror**

There is little disagreement among teachers and student teachers alike in regard to the value of the conference as a method of providing growth for a teaching candidate. This face-to-face confrontation is actually where the supervisor teaches the student teacher. It is as vital to a good experience as the presence of pupils. The absence of conferences could result in no real reflection about teaching as well as the lack of any genuine information sharing.

A student teaching conference occurs when the student teacher and his supervising teacher converse in a manner which is designed to contribute to the professional growth of the student teacher. It goes beyond the inevitable conversation between supervising teacher and student teacher in that it focuses on fundamental concepts and principles related to teaching which are designed to make a difference in professional behavior. Conversation is valuable in establishing rapport and providing relaxation, but a conference is essential in guiding the educational progress of the student teacher.

There are several requisites for a successful conference. Primarily, it must be conducted in an atmosphere of mutual trust and understanding. There has to be a frankness between participants that clearly communicates a point of view or an idea. Emotions must be subservient to reason and each participant needs to have genuine respect for the other.

Timing and location of conferences are essential to success in achieving the desired objectives. The closer to the "significant moment'' that two people can confer, the better the results. Emphasis on a particular problem at the time it reaches its peak will be more effective than at any other time. An analysis of teaching will be more valuable immediately following the teaching act than it will be if it is delayed. The nature of the content of a conference is such that the student teacher and supervising teacher should confer privately. An interruption by a third party can be distracting to both student teacher and supervising teacher. Even the mere presence of a disinterested individual can curtail openness and frank discussion.

The content of conferences will vary depending on need and the student's rate of development. In initial conferences the student teacher and supervising teacher share information; in later ones, they will give attention to analysis, reflection, and evaluation. On occasion a brief exchange is desirable in order to communicate a timely idea; other conferences need to be pre-arranged for maximum impact.

The supervising teacher has to give of himself in a conference, combining sincerity with occasional informality. He may reveal his true self and educational philosophy here more than he will in other contacts with the student teacher. He will occasionally have to make suggestions and take actions that are difficult. On these occasions, skill in the art of human relations will need to be carefully exercised. Although much is demanded of the supervising teacher as he assists the student teacher in the conference, he will receive his reward as he sees the results of his suggestions and ideas being incorporated into actions and as he sees his student teacher grow in skill effectiveness, and understanding.

The supervising teacher should help the student teacher reflect upon his experiences. It is a truism that we learn to do by doing; but if we want to accelerate our rate of learning, we must reflect upon what we do. In conferences regularly planned, the supervising teacher can help the student teacher understand his experiences. The supervising teacher must ask judicious questions. He must listen and then, and only' then, should he respond. Sometimes it may be necessary to tell the student teacher where or when he has made a mistake, but usually it is better to help him discover his own mistakes. Under no circumstances should the supervising teacher cast himself in the role of a guru doling out wisdom to the unwise.

Case Study No. 54: THE SUPERVISING TEACHER FEELS THAT HE HAS DIFFICULTY IN COMMUNICATING HIS IDEAS THROUGH A CONFERENCE

After a few conferences you have the feeling that the student teacher does not understand what you mean. She looks a bit puzzled as you talk and does not seem to respond with related ideas or questions. Furthermore, she seemed to display no evidence of having changed after you made specific recommendations. You begin to wonder if you are talking in generalizations and failing to deal specifically with relevant topics. What do you do?

1. Discuss this feeling with the student teacher
2. Seek alternative methods of communication
3. Talk the matter over with your department chairman or the college supervisor
4. Alter your conference style in order to see if some other approach is more effective
5. ──────────────────────────────────────

   Consider:

   a. The student teacher's orientation to conferences
   b. Your own understanding of what is to be communicated in a conference situation
   c. The overall rapport between you and your student teacher
   d. Reviewing conference responsibilities
   e. Other factors which could be impeding effective communication
   f. ──────────────────────────────

THE EFFECTIVE CONFERENCE: **The Mirror Elicits a Reaction**

The goal of the conference is better development in some specific aspect of the student teacher's performance. Such action may be in teaching procedure, development of plans and ideas, or the acquisition of information about school, teaching, or pupils. A conference will help the student teacher view his role more clearly and it should provide the needed direction for better action. If the student teacher goes into his tasks with new insight and assurance, the supervisor has been successful in his conference objectives.

The conference can provide a real challenge in the area of human relations. An attitude of mutual trust and respect has to prevail. If either party is reluctant to confer, a strained relationship usually results. If a student teacher fears the situation for one reason or another, his response may be negative. A poor choice of words or an ill-chosen expression can create unnecessary tension. The Association for Student Teaching makes several suggestions in its bulletin relating to supervisory conferences:[1]

The supervising teacher must learn to listen
   Do not get so busy formulating responses that you fail to listen to what is being said

1 Association for Student Teaching, **Supervisory Conference as Individualized Teaching,** Bulletin No. 28, 1969, pp. 25-29.

Try to meet the needs expressed by the student teacher
Information
Reassurance
Evaluative comments
Understand how the student teacher feels in the situation
At best he is insecure--at worst he is actually frightened
Maintain objectivity during conferences
Emphasis should be placed on what actually was said and done
rather than on opinions of what occurred

Conferences should be concerned with matters which are felt to be important. The student teacher will be interested in the analysis of his performance after he has taught. An incident with a pupil will find the student teacher receptive to discussion of the technique he used in managing the situation. Confusion about responsibility or procedure can provide the basis for a conference on requirements and duties of the student teacher. Occasionally the supervising teacher may need to call attention to topics that should be discussed and certainly the student teacher will constantly be raising questions.

Most worthwhile conferences are dependent upon the extent to which the participants are prepared to discuss relevant matters. The content of a conference depends upon the needs and interests of the moment. Delay in conferring may result in significant information being discussed too late for the student teacher to take any remedial action. In other instances, it may result in the actual impact being lost due to the passing of time. The supervisor must be alert for the "conferrable moment" with the student teacher just as he is for the "teachable moment" in working with a group of pupils.

The regular conference will provide systematic communication between supervising teacher and student teacher. Contrary to the beliefs of some supervisors, the conference is not designed only to solve problems. An effective conference does not destroy the student's confidence or cause rapport to deteriorate. Frequent looks at teaching ideas and problems will help the student teacher to view the supervisor as a resource person who is seriously interested in him and in his development.

The student teacher is anxious for feedback concerning his progress. Lack of such regular communication often leads to suspicion and causes the student teacher to feel inadequate. If the supervising teacher fails to provide any breakdown regarding the experience, the student teacher may feel that he is not performing satisfactorily and that the supervisor does not want to embarrass him with frequent criticisms. Or he may feel that he is being exploited and the supervising teacher is really not interested in him. This is probably contrary to the supervising teacher's intentions, but the absence of communication through conferences contributes to a deterioration of rapport and understanding.

Topics generally discussed in comprehensive conferences include:

Analysis of teaching skills
    Verbal interaction
    Nonverbal communication
    Manipulation of subject matter
    Emotional rapport with pupils
Evaluation of the student teacher's progress
    What teaching and learning is taking place
    Particular skills of the student teacher
    Helping the student teacher formulate a concept of good
        teaching and how he compares with that concept
    Specific suggestions for overcoming weaknesses
Information about the school
    School policies for teachers
    Rules and regulations for students
    Curricular organization
    Availability of and procedures for securing resources
    Role of specialized personnel
    Reports and records
    General questions about the school
Information about students
    Test records
    Personal information
    Unique circumstances which might affect learning
Sharing teacher's ideas and knowledge
    Philosophy of teaching
    Philosophy of grading and evaluation
    Ideas concerning discipline
    Techniques of keeping records
    Suggestions concerning planning and organization
    Gathering resource material
    How to improvise
    Dealing with emergencies
    Professional organizations
    Arranging for field trips and resource personnel
    Why a situation or problem was handled in a certain manner
Discussion of plans for teaching
    Pre-teaching analysis
    Post-teaching appraisal
    Long-range plans and ideas
    Discussion of possible activities and techniques
Defining goals
    Classroom goals
    Teaching progress

Personal adjustment of the student teacher
    Personal problems as they relate to the school setting
    Relations with colleagues or pupils
    Personal values
    Personal mannerisms
    Attitudes toward people

Initial Conferences

Initial conferences normally provide opportunities for a student teacher and his supervising teacher to get acquainted and for orientation of the two participants to their respective roles and opportunities. The teaching candidate may feel uneasy in this new situation, and the supervising teacher can also have some feeling of uncertainty. The initial conference can establish a mutual bond and working relationship between the two. The supervising teacher must be cognizant of the fact that the student teacher has been thrust into a situation that is different from the university environment and that he will need assistance in making transition to his new role. If such assistance is to be effectively rendered, it will be necessary for the supervising teacher to learn as much as he can about the student teacher. He will also want to query the student teacher about supervisory practices or guidelines recommended by the university.

This discussion is recommended even if the supervising teacher is thoroughly informed of these practices himself, for it offers an opportunity to emphasize these points to the student teacher. The following agenda can be highly functional for the initial conference or conferences. The student teacher will want to know:

What role he is to perform
What his responsibilities will be
What he is to do during the first few days of class
The location of supplies and materials
Information about the classes he is to teach
Pertinent information about the school and community
Something about the supervising teacher's philosophy and teaching
    style

The supervising teacher will want to explore:

The student teacher's academic background
The student teacher's interests and experiences
The university student teaching requirements
Personal information about the student teacher

Frequency of Conferences

Much important discourse can occur in brief exchanges between the supervising teacher and the student teacher that focus on present interests or problems. Ideally, a conference should occur whenever it is needed. For example, a brief critique of a lesson immediately after it has been taught can be of greater significance than waiting for a period of time before the analysis is conducted.

The brief, informal conference keeps the lines of communication open at all times. If teacher and student teacher are accustomed to being receptive to each other continually, they will find themselves discussing topics as they are relevant. This informal procedure also has the distinct advantage of creating a less threatening environment for the discussion of the inevitable questions that arise when two individuals work together as student teacher and supervisor.

In addition to the spontaneous, informal conferences, the supervising teacher and student teacher can plan for a time periodically when they may confer without interruption. This arrangement can assist the supervising teacher in that it gives him the occasion to discuss planning in detail as well as to share information and ideas. This procedure is especially valuable when the student teacher is timid or insecure as it forces him to come into direct interaction with the supervising teacher.

Case Study No. 55: THE AGREEABLE, BUT UNCHANGING STUDENT TEACHER

Your student teacher is as cooperative in his conversation as one would want. The problem is that he seldom follows through on any of the points which have been agreed upon. In spite of your efforts, he just continues to agree with you and then proceeds as if you had never talked. What do you do in this situation?

1. If it involves agreement on concrete items such as the submission of plans, refuse to let him proceed with activity until he meets the conditions previously agreed upon
2. Instead of asking him to agree, force him to make statements or comments and then concur with him
3. Be more demanding in following through when conditions are not met
4. Write agreements down so there is a concrete record
5. ————————————————————————————

Consider:

a. The cause for this inconsistent behavior
b. Whether you are communicating as you feel you are
c. Learning more about the student teacher's background in order to learn how he has responded to other situations
d. ————————————————————

Case Study No. 56: THE DEFENSIVE STUDENT TEACHER

The conference period had been a strained period between you and the student teacher from the very beginning. You felt that he perceived that you were prying even in your early endeavors to explore his background and to determine where his major interests lay. Now that he has started teaching, your attempts at analyzing the lesson seem to bring negative reactions. He indicates that he is doing satisfactory work and implies that there is nothing which needs to be talked about. When criticisms or suggestions for improvement are made, he states that he does not agree and says that he is teaching the way he was instructed by university methods teachers. Since little progress is being made, what course of action do you take?

1. Abandon such conferences as they are obviously failing
2. Try to revise your procedure and become more indirect
3. Be quite frank and inform him that he should make an honest effort to change before it is too late
4. Be selective for a while and concentrate only on topics where some agreement or consensus can be reached
5. _____

Consider:

a. Procedures to cause the student teacher to be more open in his discussions with you
b. The content which is necessary in a conference
c. _____

Case Study No. 57: THE STUDENT TEACHER AVOIDS SCHEDULED CONFERENCES

One of your major difficulties has been the problem of getting your student teacher to participate in conferences. He seems to find other things to do during conference time or indicates that he does not have any questions. When you do manage to sit down together, he gives perfunctory answers to your questions and comments and attempts to steer you into conversation about topics which are not directly related to his student teaching. Since you are convinced that conferences are necessary, what do you do?

1. Arrange a specific time each day for conferences and have an agenda of topics for discussion
2. Attempt to structure these sessions so that the student teacher does not feel uncomfortable in participation
3. State the reasons for the conferences so that he will understand the rationale guiding these sessions
4. Abandon any further attempts until he makes some gesture indicating interest
5. _____

Consider:

a. Examining the reason the student avoids conferences
b. Alternative methods of communication
c. The relationship between you and the student teacher and how he perceives that relationship
d. _____

The class terminated and Brian had a period of time to confer with Miss Bennett. He was anxious to know what she thought of his procedure, especially since he planned to utilize the same technique in subsequent lessons if it was considered effective.

They sat down at the desk and began talking. Brian was cautiously optimistic as he began, "I thought they showed more interest than usual and they seemed to handle the discussion questions with more insight than I had expected."

Miss Bennett agreed, "I felt that they were able to comprehend the reasons behind the questions and they had read enough to have some supportive facts available. What did you think of your introduction?"

Brian thought, and slowly responded, "I guess it was not too good."

Miss Bennett responded, "But it was not all bad. Why did you think it wasn't good?"

Brian quickly replied, "They didn't pay close attention and it could have been difficult for them to see how it related to the later questions."

She inquired, "How could it have been made better?"

Brian considered the question and then speculated that an actual tape recording of the event or some dramatic statement might have commanded more thinking.

Miss Bennett accepted his evaluation and further stated, "You might use the board to list important ideas, too. One other point, did you notice that you directed most of the questions to about five students -- Jo, Jan, Donna, Rex, and Tom?"

"Did I?" exclaimed a surprised Brian. "Now that I think of it, I believe that is right. I will have to go beyond those who are wanting to talk all the time."

Miss Bennett smiled and then gave an endorsement to Brian's technique which he had tried for the first time. The conference drifted into conversation, and they left feeling that the session had been productive.

Remember:

A conference should involve the free flow of ideas which will foster an objective analysis of the development and improvement of the student teacher's competencies.

Any conference should be problem-centered instead of person-centered

A conference should be constructive, with the student teacher feeling that he has received help or that it has enabled him to become more self-directive

A conference should be private

A good conference should lead to concrete plans of action which are useful in guiding future activities

The conference is the period of time when the supervisor interacts most effectively with the student teacher

Frequent conferences are less threatening than infrequent conferences
Conferences should be concerned with matters considered to be important by their participants
Conferences should lead to satisfaction on the part of the participants

USEFUL REFERENCES

ASSOCIATION FOR STUDENT TEACHING, *Guiding Student Teaching Experiences,* Association for Student Teaching Bulletin No. 1, 1968, pp. 16-17
    Guidelines for building effective conferences
    Topics and situations discussed in the conference
    Frequency of conferences
ASSOCIATION FOR STUDENT TEACHING, Supervisory Conference as Individualized Teaching, Association for Student Teaching Bulletin No. 28, 1969
    Importance of the conference
    Principles of effective conferences
    Rewards of productive conferences
GOLDHAMMER, ROBERT, *Clinical Supervision,* Holt, Rinehart, and Winston, 1969, Chapter 6
    Methods of the conference
KYTE, GEORGE C., "Establishing Rapport in the Supervisory Conference," *The Educational Forum* 28:317-323, November, 1963
STRATEMEYER, FLORENCE, AND LINDSEY, MARGARET, *Working With Student Teachers,* Teachers College Press, Columbia University, New York, 1958, Chapter 14
    Types of conferences and their purposes
    Major areas of discussion in conferences
    Essentials of the effective conference
SWEARINGEN, MILDRED E., *Supervision of Instruction: Foundations and Dimensions,* Allyn and Bacon, Inc., 1962, Chapter 6
TELFER, HAROLD E., AND SLEEPER, WILLIAM R., "The Student Teaching Conference: A Must," *Peabody Journal of Education* 41:169-172, November, 1963
WILES, KIMBALL, *Supervision for Better Schools,* Prentice-Hall, 1967, Chapter 5
    Application of communication theory to supervisory practices

Chapter Nine

SUPERVISING PARTICIPATION IN THE TOTAL SCHOOL PROGRAM

It had been one of those long, dreary days when nothing had gone as planned. A fire alarm interrupted the timed examination, needed materials did not get duplicated as promised, Linda and Cristie had a big argument in class, and it had now started to rain outside. As dismissal time approached, a voice sounded on the intercom, "Teachers are reminded of the Open House tonight. Faculty members should be in their rooms by 7:00 o'clock."

"The end of a perfect day," commented Miss Bennett in her droll manner. "Did they tell you about this in methods class?"

Brian forced a smile. The last thing he wanted to do was to return for the Open House. He had about two hours of paperwork and he had hoped to relax a bit after that. The Open House would eliminate that completely. Turning toward the window, he inquired, "Do you think it would be all right if I did not attend tonight? I completely forgot about this and I had planned to get together with some friends later this evening after I finished grading the tests. Since I attended the PTA meeting last month and met several parents, I wonder if I might be excused from this one."

Miss Bennett considered the dilemma. She could appreciate his point of view. He had been working hard and she knew the relaxation was well deserved, especially after this trying day. She was also aware of the fact that the school administration was stressing "loyalty" to this program in order to encourage more parental participation by assuring them that the teachers would be present. Brian probably should meet some of these parents.

Miss Bennett took a quick check of the gray skies outside and softly inquired, "What did they tell you at State? Do they expect you to attend?"

"I don't remember that it was ever discussed," was Brian's instant response.

PARTICIPATION IN THE TOTAL SCHOOL PROGRAM: School Does Not End at 3:30

Teacher education programs made significant progress when they began to require a full day's student teaching experience in the school. This innovation enabled the teacher candidate to devote complete attention to living the life of a teacher. The "block arrangement" has allowed a student teacher to participate in the total program of activities of the school both during and after the school day. The result has been that student teachers are afforded an opportunity to see pupils in a manner which was previously impossible. Student teachers have developed a more comprehensive view of the responsibilities of a teacher through this association with the diverse school activity program.

Participation gives the student teacher an opportunity for total involvement in school affairs. This kind of experience permits a new type of interaction with both teachers and pupils which may be more fulfilling than the contact during the school day. The reserved student teacher, for instance, may feel more at ease in the informal situations where rapport can be established more easily. Informal interaction with youth allows student teachers to see a side of the pupils that they are not otherwise able to see. One student teacher commented that she really got to know her students when she worked with them on the construction of a float for the homecoming parade. If a teacher candidate capitalizes on opportunities of this type, he can get to know some of his students better. This enriching opportunity can help him adjust more easily to pupils in the formal learning situations. It may cause more favorable reaction from pupils in that they may perceive that the student teacher has a genuine interest in them because he voluntarily attended their activities.

The participation experience is an opportunity for the student teacher to make a contribution to the school through the utilization of particular competencies which he may possess. For example, a student teacher with musical talent may be able to assist a student with his practice; a physical education major may be able to contribute his athletic skills to coaching; and a student teacher who has had experience directing group activities may be of value to pupils who are presenting a program to a school assembly or community organization.

Exposure to the school and community can best be achieved through participation. Administrators, particularly, may have little opportunity to see the student teacher except through the contacts of professional and extracurricular activities. Other teachers and school personnel will have their best opportunities to know the student teacher in these situations. Most of the community members will never see a student teacher unless he is visible at some school function. From the educational point of view, it must be recognized that student teachers can learn much about teaching through participation. Attendance at faculty meetings and participation in home rooms, for example, may give student teachers a glimpse of professional skills and techniques that had never before occurred to them.

Unless the student participates in the entire scope and range of professional activities, he may not gain a valid knowledge and understanding of the entire school program and the contribution it makes. Many a student teacher will feel honored at being invited to take part in school activities outside the classroom. Such an invitation helps make him an important person in his own right and not just a classroom lackey.

Participation will help the student teacher:

Get to know and understand his pupils
Understand the types of learning that take place outside the classroom
   social learning
   skills

Understand the demands that are made upon a teacher
Meet and interact with parents and other adults in the community
Work with other teachers
Learn about the purposes and functions of the school
Understand the role of professional organizations in teaching

Case Study No. 58: THE STUDENT TEACHER IS RELUCTANT TO PARTICIPATE IN AFTER-SCHOOL ACTIVITIES

Ron commutes to your school each day from his apartment near the campus, a distance of twenty-five miles one way. He is also actively involved in the social and political affairs of the university. He appears to be enjoying his teaching and his progress is satisfactory, but he has seen very little of school life after hours. When you suggest that he participate in some of these functions, he indicates a willingness to do so, but says the expense of the second trip and certain campus activities make it nearly impossible. What course of action do you take?

1. Accept his explanation and cease to ask him to participate
2. Inform him that student teaching is not complete until he has experienced the informal portions of the school day
3. Attempt to get him involved in some activity where he will be needed or rewarded
4. Discuss the requirements for participation with the college supervisor
5. _____

Consider:

a. The nature of the activities
b. The ultimate implication upon his ability to teach successfully
c. The contributions he can make in various activities
d. The requirements of the university
e. _____

Case Study No. 59: THE STUDENT TEACHER REQUESTS REMUNERATION FOR AFTER-SCHOOL SESSIONS

You are convinced of the value of a student teacher's experiencing all aspects of a teacher's life, both exciting and routine. Thus, when you are asked to collect tickets at an athletic function, you feel that this would be a good activity for your student teacher to experience. When you ask him to do so, he indicates that he will provided he is paid at the same rate as the other teachers who are working. You explain that this is a learning experience, but he counters with the statement that he is learning to teach but this is merely an experience which requires labor and he feels he should be compensated.

Assuming there is some compensation involved, what do you decide to do?

1. Inform him that he can collect the compensation you would normally receive
2. Indicate that there is as much opportunity to learn in this situation as there is in the classroom
3. Tell him that he does not need to participate
4. _____

   Consider:

   a. The contrast between learning experiences and utilization of services
   b. The basic reason for his participating in such an activity
   c. Financial needs of college students
   d. _____

PARTICIPATION ACTIVITIES: **Educational Smorgasbord**

The range of activities is usually extensive in the school where student teachers are assigned. Obviously the student teacher will not be able to see and do everything in the few weeks that he is in the school, so priorities will need to be determined in order to utilize time to best advantage. Those activities that will be of most benefit in helping the student teacher learn about teaching should be of primary concern. Secondly, responsibilities should be provided which are normally expected of a teacher, so that the student teacher may get to experience activities which he will be responsible for in the future.

Although there is no one pattern of activities that is tailored for all situations, the following list represents those experiences in which student teachers are usually involved:

Faculty duties related to instruction
    Faculty meetings
    Supervision of hall corridors and cafeteria
    Homeroom responsibilities
    Completion of reports and other information required by the school
    Parent conferences
    Attendance at parent-teacher meetings, open houses, and other school functions
    Additional instructional assistance to individual students
    After-school rehearsals and practices
    Conferences and meetings with administrative and supervisory personnel
    Collecting fees and money
Professional activities
    Meetings of professional organizations

Conferences
Committee assignments
Extracurricular functions
Supervision of clubs
Attendance at athletic contests, plays, and musicals
Chaperone dances and other social activities
Attend faculty social functions
Work at athletic games and other programs

Participation in faculty affairs gives the student teacher the impression that he is accepted and presents a real way in which he can be involved. These kinds of experiences illustrate the professional skills utilized by teachers out of the classroom as well as demonstrate the method in which a teacher interacts with staff and other people associated with the school.

The student teacher generally will not have any valid concept of the role of professional organizations, as professional content courses may give only a cursory treatment of their contributions to education. Student teaching may provide the first real opportunity for the teaching candidate to observe the role of such groups.

The college background of a student teacher may help him to be a real contributor to extracurricular programs. His talents in such fields as athletics and music can be utilized in the more informal curricular functions. School officials and pupils alike appreciate the fact that a student teacher volunteers to participate in extracurricular activities. They perceive that it is an index of interest and dedication to teaching, and pupils feel that they get to know the student teacher better and that he has an interest in them personally.

Case Study No. 60: THE STUDENT TEACHER TAKES CHARGE IN A PARENT CONFERENCE

Since scheduled conferences with parents occur during the time that you have a student teacher, you decide to ask her to participate in those sessions. She was eager for the experience and even more eager in the conversations with parents. During one conference with a mother whose child she has been helping with in compensatory work, she completely takes charge. The mother looks a bit confused and you fear that your student teacher might not properly interpret some delicate bits of information concerning the pupil. What do you do?

1. Explain that your student teacher has had considerable training at college and her contribution has been significant as far as the child is concerned
2. Withdraw from the conversation and take the role of an observer but remind yourself that there should be an evaluative follow-up to this conversation

3. Find an excuse to distract the student teacher so that you can gain the initiative
4. Deliberately force yourself into the conference until you gain control
5. _____

   Consider:

   a. The possibility that confidential information might be revealed
   b. The impact upon a student teacher if he is relegated to a subordinate position
   c. Techniques of effecting a team approach to such conferences
   d. The necessity of prior analysis before a parent is confronted
   e. _____

Case Study No. 61: THE STUDENT TEACHER CRITICIZES PROFESSIONAL ORGANIZATIONS

You and your student teacher have just left a meeting of your local teachers' association. It had been a long day and admittedly the meeting that day had not been the most exciting. After you talk a bit, your student teacher asks why you bother to participate in such a bland group. Don't teachers have enough to do without attending useless meetings of organizations which just extract money from the teachers? Furthermore, she wants to know what this organization ever did for young teachers. How do you react to her accusations?

1. Attempt to cite briefly the accomplishments of a professional organization
2. Ask her to get to know the organization better before final judgment is made
3. Explain that the organization is not perfect, but that it does have a potential to make a positive contribution to education in general
4. _____

   Consider:

   a. A method of systematically exposing a student teacher to a professional organization
   b. The ethical response to such an accusation
   c. Formulation of a procedure to communicate the real value of such an organization
   d. _____

Case Study No. 62: RESPONDING TO A STUDENT TEACHER'S IMMATURE BEHAVIOR AT A SCHOOL MIXER

The school mixer seemed to be a logical activity for Dennis to supervise since you had the responsibility for this particular dance. It soon became apparent, however, that you had just one more person to supervise instead of having an assistant. A few

of the pupils gathered around him for a long time and he was enjoying the attention. Whatever he was saying to them certainly
was amusing and he seemingly relished their attention. The final
challenge came when he began to dance with one of the girls.
You are aware of the danger of too much fraternization but he
obviously is not. How do you react to this situation?

1. Find some responsibility that he can perform which will
   get him involved in a constructive manner
2. Call him aside and explain the possible consequences if
   he continues with his present actions
3. Ignore the situation at present, but later explain the
   possible consequences of his behavior
4. Attempt to redirect the mixer into an activity where the
   student teacher will not be so vulnerable
5. _____

   Consider:

   a. The best method of communicating with a student
      teacher in such situations
   b. Methods of effectively redirecting the student
      teacher's interests
   c. The ethical position of both you and the student
      teacher
   d. _____

THE SUPERVISING TEACHER'S ROLE IN DIRECTING PARTICIPATION EXPERIENCES: **Interpreting the Menu**

The world beyond the classroom may not be as readily apparent to
the student teacher as the classroom environment. Little conscious attention is given to it in his professional preparation, and he may be only
vaguely aware of a teacher's duties as he recalls his years as a pupil.
Activities such as faculty and professional meetings may have escaped
him completely. Since most of the participation activities are non-credit
for pupils and constitute additional demands on teachers, the student
teacher may need to be made aware of the requirements of teachers for
contributions after school.

The student teacher might also have little or no frame of reference
in regard to the priorities he should place upon participation. He will
depend upon the supervising teacher to acquaint him with the various
activities and to suggest appropriate responsibilities for him to assume.
The following might serve as a checklist for consideration in guiding the
student teacher's activities in participation:

*Explanation of what is expected from the student teacher by way of par-
   ticipation*
   Discussion of student teacher interests
   Indication of teacher's own responsibilities

Normal expectations of teachers in participation activities
   Requirements as part of contractual obligation
Possibilities for extension of classroom work
   Clubs
   Programs
Scheduling of events
   Who schedules
   Where they are scheduled
Guidelines or rules covering the various activities
Opportunities for learning through participation
Opportunities for contribution

The supervisor's responsibility could be described as that of informing and guiding. He assumes the responsibility of seeing that the student teacher is made aware of the number of activities which consume a teacher's out-of-class time. He then attempts to involve the student teacher in those situations which will be of value to him and which, hopefully, make a direct contribution.

Dr. Phillips was admitted to the principal's office prior to his supervisory visit to Brian's class. After a few preliminary remarks, he inquired about Brian's progress as a student teacher. The principal stated that he was doing quite well and that he was a good representative of the university. He observed that Brian was one of the few student teachers who attended the Open House the other evening and that he is always looking for contributions which he can make. He thought it was a good indication of interest that he stayed around after school instead of rushing to the parking lot to get away as soon as he could. He went on to comment that he could not make any valid appraisals of his teaching skill, but what he had seen of him made him think that Mr. Sims was doing well in the classroom, too.

Dr. Phillips indicated appreciation of the report as he scribbled a few notes for his records.

Remember:

The student teacher should be involved in the same kinds of activities as the regular teacher

Participation helps the student teacher feel that he is accepted and needed

Student teachers are exposed to a wider audience in participation activity than in a classroom activity

Participation alone is not enough - reflection and discussion with the supervising teacher make a real difference in the value of the experience for the student teacher

USEFUL REFERENCES

BATCHELDER, HOWARD T., McGLASSON, MAURICE, AND SCHORLING, RALEIGH, *Student Teaching in Secondary Schools*, McGraw-Hill, 1964, Chapter 13
    The teacher in the student activity program
CURTIS, DWIGHT K., AND ANDREWS, L. O., *Guiding Your Student Teacher*, Prentice-Hall, 1954, Chapter 10
    Preparing the student teacher to assume responsibilities in extraclass activities
    Supervising the student teacher in extraclass activities
DEVOR, JOHN W., *The Experience of Student Teaching*, Macmillan, 1964, Chapter 5
    Participation in routine and extraclass activities
STRATEMEYER, FLORENCE, AND LINDSEY, MARGARET, *Working With Student Teachers*, Teachers College Press, Columbia University, New York, 1958, Chapter 12
    Experiences in guiding classroom activities
    Experience with the total school organization
    Experience with the teacher's role in the community

Chapter Ten

SUPERVISING THE PROBLEM STUDENT TEACHER

Miss Bennett left Central City early with two of her colleagues for the drive to State University, where she and the other cooperating teachers for that school had been invited to attend a conference for supervising teachers. She welcomed the opportunity because she would meet other teachers who worked with student teachers as well as university personnel connected with the teacher preparation program. It would be the first occasion for her to communicate with teachers from other schools and she looked forward to learning more about the process of supervision. The supervising teachers had been requested to bring any problems to a group discussion focusing on difficulties that they were experiencing in working with their student teachers. She concluded that this particular session would be of little interest since she could see no cause for quandry in working with a student teacher. How wrong she was!

As soon as the chairman opened the meeting for discussion, there was a barrage of complaints and pleas for assistance. One teacher commented that her student teacher was lazy, and another complained that his student teacher was so busy with work and campus activities that he missed several days and was usually unprepared when he was in school. Miss Bennett shifted in her seat as she heard another teacher describe her student teacher's "contemporary appearance," and she was really surprised to hear that two supervisors had been faced with the problem of student teachers who were absolutely incapable of working with pupils.

"You are all lucky," commented one teacher who had remained silent up to this point. "My student teacher proceeded to tell the class how easy it was to make a drug called 'mellow yellow' from banana peels and said that it couldn't hurt you 'very much.' On another occasion she said (when explaining the fertilization of the human egg), 'You have to be careful in the cycle when the egg is in the Fallopian tube or you could possibly get pregnant.' " The discussion time elapsed before all of the problems could be identified, not to mention being solved. Miss Bennett left the room wondering what she would do if she were faced with a problem student teacher . . .

The vast majority of student teachers will prove to be mature thinking individuals capable of assuming adult responsibilities and contributing to a more effective learning climate. With very few exceptions, they will be highly motivated and eager to gain as much as they can from student teaching. The supervising teacher who adheres to the normal pattern of supervision will experience a pleasant relationship with his student teacher in almost every case.

In spite of the best programs of university preparation, screening, and orientation to student teaching, some students will enter the professional semester unable to cope with the demands of teaching. If a real problem does develop, it can cause a great amount of concern and consume a tremendous amount of time and energy on the part of the cooperating teacher. This chapter recognizes some of the more typical problems and suggests some alternative procedures which could be pursued until a more comprehensive solution can be reached by all individuals concerned.

THE STUDENT TEACHER WHO REJECTS THE ESTABLISHMENT: **Discomfort on Both Sides of the Glass House**

The prevailing values of public school personnel often conflict with the current life styles and ideas of our younger citizens in teacher education. Attempts at communication or reconciliation must be carefully executed or they may breach the gap instead of close it. The villain in the drama is the individual who chooses to pursue unilateral action without involving or considering the other party. Student teaching can be the arena of confrontation in the generation gap.

In a sense, a college student is sheltered from the school's value system, and the student teacher may enter the classroom unaware that his ideas, values, and habits may be challenged by the administration of that school. His life as a student is normally one of intellectual and personal independence where he is encouraged to be an individual and to be a social critic. Furthermore, he may not be aware that many of his beliefs and actions are contrary to the operating style of a school. Habits of appearance and dress, for example, that are acceptable on campus may be unacceptable in the public school. The student who is acquainted with the candid, direct method of bringing about change may come in conflict with the administrator who insists that requests be made through "appropriate channels." Actions of student teachers may be perceived as defiance when they are actually merely following the life style of the college environment.

The student teacher probably views himself as a college student rather than as a teacher. One girl commented to the author that she was surprised to learn that her pupils considered her to be part of the "Establishment." She did not feel that she was a part of this system, and she was not certain that she wanted to be. School personnel, too, may regard the student teacher as a "rebel" and may be very concerned about the actions and ideas of this "alien."

The ideals and operating style of the student teacher potentially might terminate in a direct conflict with the practices and policies of the school system. Differences of opinion range from trivia ("His hair is too long") to relevant social issues (the role of the citizen in affecting change in a democracy.) Typical differences of opinion arise in regard to:

Hair styles
Skirt lengths
Type of clothing worn
Civil rights

Methods and techniques of dissent
Morality
Role and policies of the government
Social issues
Personal relationships with pupils

The differences are not impossible to reconcile. The method of communication is probably the critical variable in reaching accord when divergent views exist. If a student teacher is ordered to change his appearance or behavior without a reasonable explanation hostility is nearly inevitable. However, if the supervising teacher or principal discusses the policy with the student teacher, he may be more inclined to be cooperative in spite of the fact that he does not accept the rationale. Consideration of the following points can help in creating a better understanding:

The student teacher is accepted as a person and not rejected solely on the basis of his appearance or belief
Any explanation of a policy should include why it is in existence
Double standards should not be applied to student teachers and regular teachers
Ignoring some behaviors can frequently solve the problem better than emphasizing the consequences of non-compliance
Discussions of concepts related to rules might enlarge an individual's perspective
   Each person surrenders some liberty to be a member of a group
   Change can occur through evolution as well as revolution
   Present rules as necessary for the effective operation of a system

The supervising teacher is in a position to help reconcile the existing differences or to inform the student teacher of expected change. He can also find himself working with the student teacher in his adjustment to the new environment or in effectively promoting his point of view.

Case Study No. 63: THE STUDENT TEACHER REFUSES TO PLEDGE ALLEGIANCE TO THE FLAG

You have suggested that your student teacher visit a club meeting which is sponsored by a fairly conservative teacher. Each session of the group begins with the Pledge of Allegiance. Your student teacher stands, but does not recite the pledge. The sponsor notes this and immediately confronts you with the incident and demands that he pay proper respect. The incident is referred to the principal who considers removing the student teacher from the school. You discuss the incident with the student teacher and he admits that as a matter of conscience he does not believe in reciting the Pledge of

Allegiance. When informed of his possible removal from student teaching, he says that if he is told to leave he will contact the Civil Liberties Union and possibly initiate legal action against the school. As the student's supervising teacher, what do you do?

1. Inform the principal of his belief and intention
2. Suggest to the principal that he be allowed to remain and that you will see that he will not again be in a position where he will be present when the Pledge of Allegiance is given
3. Demand that he conform to school policies
4. Indicate that you understand his point of view, but suggest that he alter his behavior in order to complete his student teaching
5. Discuss the matter with him and attempt to help him reconcile his position with the school's requirements
6. Call the college supervisor and ask him to resolve the situation
7. _____

   Consider:

   a. Methods of reconciling the conflict which might be satisfactory to both school and student teacher
   b. Alternatives available to the student teacher
   c. The validity of the school's request
   d. _____

Case Study No. 64: THE STUDENT TEACHER DELIBERATELY IGNORES A REQUEST

Your student teacher has been working with some inner city pupils in planning a program for Black History Week. This program was to be presented to the entire student body in an auditorium program. The plan was for the session to be concluded by having the group sing one of the contemporary songs which was closely identified with the Black movement. The principal asks you to request that he eliminate the song because it might incite discontent. Your student teacher strongly disagrees, but he is told that it will have to be eliminated. The program proceeds well and according to plan, except at the conclusion the student teacher directs the assembled group in the singing of the controversial song. A glance at the principal indicates that his anger will not be restrained. What do you do?

1. Inform the student teacher that he has violated instructions and that he will likely be dismissed as a student teacher
2. Seek to evaluate the results of the new song and concur in disciplinary action only if the song does cause confusion in the school
3. Attempt to explain the reasons why the student teacher was not to include the song and ask him to explain his reasons for violating instructions
4. _____

Consider:

a. Analysis of the merit of the request and of the
   student's action
b. The effect of ignoring an administrative order
c. Techniques of preventing direct confrontation
d. ───────────────────────────────

THE INCOMPETENT STUDENT TEACHER: **Looking at the Worst, Hoping for the Best**

In a small percentage of cases, it is obvious that the normal term of student teaching will not be sufficient to warrant a recommendation for a teaching certificate. Making decisions on incompetence is difficult, but the recent emphasis on specific skills of teaching is making it simpler to identify and describe teaching deficiencies as well as pedagogical strengths. Incompetency is likely to be determined if weaknesses exist in various areas. An extreme lack in any one of the following traits could lead to a possible determination of inadequacy:

Personal deficiency
　　Extremely timid
　　Immature
　　Problems of mental health
　　Failure to establish workable personal relationships with
　　　pupils, teachers and auxiliary school personnel
Lack of organizational skills
　　Ineffective planning
　　Failure to meet responsibilities
Lack of interest in teaching
Inability to work with people
　　Cannot cooperate with a supervisor
　　Cannot establish rapport with pupils
Inability to communicate
Inability to manage a classroom independently
　　Pupils cooperate only through coercion by the supervising
　　　teacher
　　Student teacher has to ask for help or suggestions after several
　　　weeks of student teaching have elapsed
Unable to evaluate himself realistically
　　Refuses to evaluate himself
　　Estimates are too high
　　Appraisals are too low
*Unable to structure the environment in such a way that learning
　occurs*
　　No apparent change of behavior on the part of students
　　Little or no evidence of increased knowledge

Fails to provide the proper technique for the specific learning task

Seems to have little or no concept of the function of a school

Does not understand the social context of the school environment

Seems to have no considered philosophy of education

Cannot see the relationship or importance of the various facets of the school program

Does not seem to possess the essential skills of teaching

Asking questions

Utilization of media and resources

Knowledge of use of common techniques of instruction

Concept of method

Many of the above weaknesses can be improved through recognition and concentrated effort. If the problem is identified early and the student teacher is aware of it, a successful plan may be devised which would lead to progress toward amelioration. Although each problem needs an individual diagnosis and plan of action, the following procedures seem to have broad application in helping the incompetent student teacher to improve.

The supervising teacher works in closer proximity with the student teacher

Remains in the room

Assists him when needed

Is present in informal contacts with pupils and teachers whenever possible

Asks the student teacher to share activities so that he might get a better concept of what is involved

The student teacher and supervising teacher work together in classes

Team arrangements with limited responsibility

The supervising teacher insists on thorough planning and requests that plans be presented far enough in advance so that review and revision can be made

Shares ideas for planning and teaching procedure

The student teacher assumes full responsibility more gradually

He is given tasks where success can logically be expected

The supervising teacher demonstrates how a task is to be achieved

The supervising teacher inquires about other activities that might be competing for a student teacher's time

If there are competing activities, he attempts to eliminate them

The supervising teacher provides written communication which is designed to assist the student

When it appears that little or no progress is being made through the efforts of the supervising teacher, the college supervisor should be contacted. From his more detached position, he can take the initiative in confronting the student teacher with the fact that his work is not satisfactory. His broader experience in working with student teachers can confirm the supervising teacher's doubts about the student teacher's progress. Sometimes his presence alone can be the catalyst which can bring about change. He may be able to motivate a student teacher or suggest a plan of action which will be of benefit. He may help to eliminate misconceptions by discussing problems in a three-way conference which could determine a desirable course of action.

The supervising teacher can substantiate a student teacher's poor performance with an anecdotal record. If the difficulty is such that it can be identified on tape, secure a recording of the performance for the college supervisor's use. If a video-tape-recorder is available, it can be of great value in demonstrating the absence of certain essential practices. Written information and other forms of record will give the college supervisor a better idea of what has transpired up to the present point. Just as a physician can make a better diagnosis if he knows the case history and symptoms of a patient, the supervisor can work more effectively if he has a complete record of past activities and an accurate description of deficiencies.

The greatest oversights on the part of supervisors are usually failure to keep complete records and reluctance to notify the college supervisor when incompetency is apparent. Closely behind these may be the failure to identify the problem early enough to permit a constructive attack on it during student teaching. The professional procedure is to attempt to help the student teacher improve; if this effort seems to be unsuccessful, notify the college supervisor and let him assume the responsibility for the fate of the student teacher.

Case Study No. 65: THE STUDENT TEACHER SEEMS UNABLE TO ORGANIZE AND COMMUNICATE

Bill was a phlegmatic-appearing student teacher who seemed to be unable to communicate with pupils or faculty. His low grade index adequately reflected a lack of command of subject matter. His oral presentations consisted of reading a few statements from the book. He never seemed to show any visible awareness that there was a group of students in front of him. He gave extended study periods and the students usually became bored long before the period ended. He avoided conferences whenever possible and he never had any lesson plans to present. As Bill's supervising teacher, what do you do?

1. Discuss all weaknesses with him point by point

2. Ask the college supervisor to recall him
3. Team teach with him and delegate only responsibilities that he can execute
4. Ignore him until he comes to you
5. Ask the pupils to help him
6. _____

Consider:

a. Reasons for lack of communication
b. The amount of improvement that can logically be expected in the time designated for student teaching
c. _____

THE IMMATURE STUDENT TEACHER: **Big Man on Campus Becomes Little Boy at School**

The immature student teacher may possess all needed attributes for teaching except the ability to relate to pupils and teachers in an adult manner. His mannerisms may be amusing to the pupils and annoying to the teachers because he resorts to "college-type" vocabulary and conversation as a method of impressing others. The most aggravating immature student teacher is the presumptuous one who proceeds to explain the answers to all of man's complex problems and who is especially vociferous in describing what is wrong with education today. Other frequent symptoms of immaturity are too much informal contact with pupils and appearance that identifies with the younger set. Any good supervising teacher earns every cent of the honorarium which he is accorded for his work, but the supervisor of the immature student teacher will always have the university indebted to him.

The possibilities of overcoming the problem may not be as unlikely as the above comments would imply. A single experience or activity can often bring dramatic changes. For example, some supervising teachers have discovered that a direct "heart-to-heart" talk will achieve significant results. If the student teacher realizes that his facade is not effective, he may welcome the opportunity to abandon this strain of pretending to be someone he is not.

Several indirect procedures can be employed in supervision of the immature student teacher which can often be successful:

Initiate tactics designed to help the student teacher be accepted as an adult by both pupils and faculty
Place rather demanding responsibilities upon him
    If he is successful, he may volitionally abandon some of his immature ways
    If he fails, he may experience a sobering reaction

*Try to structure his schedule so that contact with the more immature
and insecure faculty members will be negligible*
     Conversely, encourage association with more secure teachers
*Stay close to the student teacher in situations where his immature ac-
tions are likely to be most apparent*
Expect and demand real contributions from him
*Assign an extensive amount of planning or project work which will be
time consuming, yet beneficial*
*Carefully supervise the student teacher's association with small groups
of individuals*
*Indicate that he has the "right" to meet the same obligations as the
teacher*
     Attendance
     Reports
     Ethics
     Relationships with pupils in general
Compliment those behaviors which show symptoms of maturity

Immaturity does not have to be a permanent condition. The alert
supervising teacher looks for opportunities to accelerate the process of
maturation. The environment should be conducive to causing the
student teacher to abandon his immature practices and to acquire a
more responsible role.

Case Study No. 66: THE STUDENT TEACHER SEEKS THE
COMPANIONSHIP OF PUPILS

Your student teacher has an adequate command of his subject knowledge and possesses acceptable skills of teaching.
The only serious problem is that of fraternization with the pupils.
He enjoys being the center of attention and the pupils give him
this opportunity readily. He spends a lot of evening hours in
situations where small groups of students congregate. They ob-
viosuly enjoy him and he is willing to spend time impressing
them. He is even seen gravitating to student company during the
school day. You have recently noticed that his classes are
becoming a bit too informal and feel that he may soon lose control because of this immature behavior. What course of action do
you take?

1. Do nothing, hoping that he will become aware of his
   behavior before too much harm is done
2. Frankly apprise him of his behavior and ask that he
   discontinue his informal conduct around students
3. Attempt to structure his schedule more rigidly so that
   fewer opportunities for fraternization exist
4. Talk to the pupils and solicit their cooperation in helping
   him become more mature
5. _____

Consider:

a. Reasons the student teacher seems to seek the company of pupils
b. The effect of such continued behavior upon the learning climate
c. ─────────────────────────────────

Case Study No. 67: THE STUDENT TEACHER WHO CANNOT ACCEPT ADULT OBLIGATIONS

Your student teacher has obviously had most of her decisions made for her. She seems to be at a complete loss in decision making, and she has sought your advice and consent for her every move. She waits to be told and does nothing if you do not give her instructions. You are beginning to wonder what she will do next year when she does not have you to depend on. What do you do in this situation?

1. Inform her that she is an adult and that you expect her to be more self-reliant
2. Continue your present pattern of supervision
3. Try to force her into more situations where she will have to make her own decisions
4. ─────────────────────────────────

Consider:

a. The reasons for this intense dependence
b. Techniques in increasing her self perception as a mature person
c. ─────────────────────────────────

Case Study No. 68: THE STUDENT TEACHER MAKES IMMATURE COMMENTS TO THE CLASS

Your student teacher had been attempting to overawe the class in a variety of ways. Each attempt seemed to cause the pupils to lose more respect for him. The incident this morning has caused the greatest concern so far. He announced to the class that he was not prepared today because he got drunk last night. He then proceeded to describe the evening and tried to impress the group by telling them what a great time he had. What do you do when this happens?

1. Take over the class immediately and indicate that since neither of you is prepared, you can probably do better because of your experience
2. Let him continue, hoping he will learn by the negative approach if his lesson fails

3. Counsel with him after class and inform him of your displeasure and indicate that further comments of that type will not be tolerated
4. Ask the pupils to write an anonymous evaluation of the class so far, assuming that they may convey ideas that will effect some change in his behavior
5. _____

   Consider:

   a. Reasons for his tendency to make such comments
   b. Techniques of preventing immature comments from being part of the lesson
   c. The effect upon the class
   d. _____

THE PROBLEM RESULTING FROM RESPONSIBILITIES BEYOND STUDENT TEACHING: **Moonlighting at Midnight**

Many of the problems affecting the student teacher have their roots in activities which consume time outside the school day. Such activities prevent the student teacher from devoting sufficient time to the teaching task. Unfortunately many of these outside diversions have deadlines and consequently their fulfillment seems more necessary than those demands of student teaching. The press of time devoted to outside responsibilities reflects in poorer teaching performance in several different ways. A student teacher highly involved in competing activities may display the following symptoms:

Inadequate preparation
Reluctance to go beyond the minimum requirements
Completion of requirements at the last minute
Absence from school
Fatigue
Boredom
Shows primary interest in affairs other than student teaching
Frequently requests to be excused from meetings
Always seems busy with non-teaching activities

Additional Course Work as a Source of Problems

The demands of an intensive college course can consume hours of valuable time. The arbitrary deadlines of an examination or a term paper can easily take preeminence over the more flexible schedule of the student teacher. The less explicit responsibilities of "gaining experience through observation" seem less important at the time than the immediate task of mastering content in preparation for a test. Students in classes compete for grades while student teaching offers either no letter grade or the implied promise of either an "A" or "B". Writing a term paper, then, seems to be more imperative than constructing a lesson plan.

If a student teacher is involved in a day-long program of teaching, he should be discouraged from enrolling in formal course work. In the event that such classes are necessary, it would be beneficial if the student teacher could relate some of the course requirements to the responsibilities of student teaching.

Part-time or Full-time Employment as a Source of Problems

The feeling of a financial necessity is a very real one to a great number of college students. Some may have completely financed their education by employment. Others obviously seek jobs in order to carry on a more affluent existence. The student teacher who has been able to work and successfully manage college responsibilities will likely anticipate that he can do the same in student teaching. He may not be prepared for the extra demand made by this laboratory experience, but he may equally be convinced of the necessity for working in order to maintain his existence.

Part-time employment is almost certainly unrelated to the professional activities of a student teacher. The immediate necessity of making payments can easily prevail over the more abstract rewards of a good student teaching experience. The conflict of demands for time can create serious problems for the student teacher.

College Activities as a Source of Problems

If the student teacher is assigned to a school close to the college campus, he may be tempted to continue with his regular pattern of social activities. Certain campus responsibilities will appear so much more imperative and desirable to him than the obligations of student teaching. Such participation competes for time as well as for intrinsic interest. Competing with the glamour of social activities can be a formidable task when a student teacher is not turned on by a room full of students. A student who is established in a social position at college may be reluctant to surrender some of that esteem to the more uncertain promises that student teaching can make, especially in regard to peer relationships.

If there is no known college policy, the supervising teacher may follow the course of least resistance and cover for the student teacher while he continues his program of campus activities. Obviously this is not the best procedure, for it only prolongs the realization that full participation is a necessity. The supervising teacher should insist that the responsibilities connected with student teaching be given first priority. If campus activities claim too much of a student teacher's time, substandard performance is all that will be displayed during the professional experience.

Adjusting to the Problems of Outside Conflicts

The student teacher has too much at stake to deliberately risk a low evaluation of his student teaching performance, though he may not realize it at the time. This evaluation, the appraisal of his experience, is secured and scrutinized by a majority of the employing officials. It is not fair to the student teacher to permit him to jeopardize this report. Consequently, when a supervising teacher feels that adequate performance is being thwarted by outside forces making demands on the student teacher's time and interest, it is suggested that he discuss the following points with the student teacher:

Learning completely about teaching cannot be accomplished by meeting the requirements at the minimum level - they must be pursued in depth.

A student teacher who is not thoroughly prepared is being unfair to the pupils he teaches

The competing demands are only temporary while the results of student teaching are permanent

The obligations of student teaching must be met; they cannot be postponed any more than a deadline in a college class or a social obligation - if the moment for learning passes, it may not reappear.

A student teacher will be unable to gain the respect of pupils or school faculty if he indicates that teaching is secondary to other activities

No other professional field permits certification or licensing without complete commitment to the profession

At this time an honest appraisal of the facts should be made and the cooperation of the student teacher solicited. Every attempt should be made to reconcile the problem so that the student teacher may not be injured, but the parties involved must be aware of the fact that a little annoyance at present can prevent greater distress in the future. When problems of this nature arise, the supervising teacher needs to be aware of the university policy in this area. If it is not covered in a student teaching handbook, the university supervisor will be able to provide this information.

Case Study No. 69: THE STUDENT TEACHER WITH PROBLEMS RESULTING FROM EMPLOYMENT

Ray had worked a great number of hours each week during his college years. This may have been part of the reason for his inadequate background in his subject. It took only a few days of student teaching to demonstrate the possibility that he might not be able to teach at the normal level expected of student teachers. In addition to his poor background, his grammar was grossly inadequate, he was not able to organize, and he had nearly lost the respect of his pupils. You realize that he will have to put in many hours of work to succeed and when you inform him of this, he says that he does not have the time because he has to work four hours at a service station each evening. He wants to teach and has been having job interviews. He says he will do better as a teacher because he will not have to work part-time. What do you do?

1. Indicate that he cannot receive credit unless his performance shows marked improvement
2. Agree that he is right and attempt to help him as much as possible by adjusting his teaching responsibilities
3. Require him to give up his job so that he can learn those skills he will need for teaching
4. Inform the college supervisor and leave the decision to him
5. _____

   Consider:

   a. Implications for the profession if substandard performance is permitted
   b. The necessity of having the funds derived from work
   c. The value of intensive learning while student teaching
   d. _____

THE PROBLEM OF UNACCEPTABLE APPEARANCE: **Failure to Wear the Uniform**

The differences between the accepted patterns of professional dress in the public schools and the prevailing pattern on the campus may create a breach that is difficult to reconcile. An administrator or a public school teacher may be concerned about the appearance of a student teacher who reflects the modes of the college community. The student teacher may be surprised to learn that his appearance is the topic of conversation because he may not be aware of the significance placed upon a more conventional dress code. Lack of discretion on the part of either the supervising teacher or the student teacher can lead to unnecessary difficulties.

Appearance problems most frequently are related to hair styles and types of clothing worn, but grooming may also be an occasional cause of concern. Male student teachers may have hair that is considered to be of the wrong length, or they may have a beard. Female student teachers may find that their skirt lengths are considered inappropriate in the school environment. Their dress may reflect the more up-to-the-moment fashion styling and schools may question whether it is acceptable.

A type of problem relating to appearance can develop if the student teacher dresses too casually. The significance of casual dress is that the young student teacher may not be distinguished in appearance from the older public school pupil. More than one student teacher has been stopped in the hall and asked for a pass slip. Such informal appearance can make it more difficult for the student teacher to be accepted by both pupils and faculty.

There is a great temptation to impose personal appearance standards upon the student teacher without giving due consideration to the fact that each individual has a right to his own taste. The supervising teacher must be careful lest he attempt to demand what he himself likes instead of insisting on standards that are necessary for achieving desirable relationships with pupils or in conforming to the standards of the school. He must be on guard to see that unreasonable or unnecessary requirements are not forced on the student teacher.

Discussing the problem of unacceptable appearance is not an easy task. The teacher may find that virtually any approach has its limitations. The following thoughts may be of benefit in formulating an approach to the problem:

The student teacher will usually prefer to have his supervising teacher discuss the subject instead of being called in by an administrator or being criticized by another teacher

An early explanation of policy can avoid an inadvertent violation of the rules

Reasons for appearance standards should be explained

Criticism of styles as such should be avoided if possible

Student teachers should not be expected to follow a dress code which is different from that of the regular faculty

Physical appearance and dress in the classroom is perhaps analogous to the procedure of wearing a uniform in other professions or positions. Wearing a uniform can lead others to assume that the wearer has certain skills, responsibilities, and authority. A certain standard of appearance as a teacher can have the same effect in teaching. If a student teacher becomes aware that appearance can help him be better accepted as a professional person with a degree of proficiency and authority, he may willingly abandon his more informal patterns of appearance.

Case Study No. 70: A DRESS THAT IS TOO SHORT

Lynn was a fairly tall girl and moderately attractive. Her student teaching assignment was in a suburban community which stressed conformity to a dress code. She apparently has failed to observe that her skirts are shorter than those of the other female teachers. The pupils do not seem to be affected by it, but the other teachers are beginning to drop hints that her appearance is not satisfactory. The principal has said nothing, but you feel that she may encounter some problems if her appearance pattern does not change. What course of action do you take?

1. Ignore the situation until it is brought to your attention by the principal or until some problem actually arises
2. Explain the situation to her and suggest that she should not let this jeopardize her good relationship with the faculty
3. Check the school regulations concerning faculty appearance and abide by its statements
4. Attempt to indirectly make her aware of the deviation
5. ───────────────────────────────────

Consider:

a. Whether this is a real problem or simply the personal preference of a few faculty members
b. The significance upon the learning environment
c. Alternative techniques of discussing the matter objectively
d. ──────────────────────────────

Case Study No. 71: THE STUDENT TEACHER UNINTENTIONALLY VIOLATES SCHOOL DRESS REGULATIONS

Your assigned student teacher made his first visit a few days before he was to begin his professional experience. Unaware of certain school rules concerning appearance, he arrived wearing a sport shirt and possessed a heavy beard. The principal said that he could not stay in that school dressed as he was and that as far as he was concerned, he could find another school for his student teaching. The student indicated that he had planned to shave, but was a member of a musical group and had two more engagements before he was to begin his student teaching. He asked if he might meet his supervising teacher as the university had requested. The principal refused, indicating that his appearance was not acceptable by school standards.

The principal informs you of the visit after the school day and expresses his distaste of his appearance. A few minutes later you are paged on the intercom to take a phone call. It is the student teacher and he wants to talk with you while he is in town since the school is some distance from the university. What do you do?

1. Suggest that the visit is not necessary and that the student teacher merely report when he is to begin his student teaching

2. Reaffirm the principal's statement and discourage him from visiting at this time so that school rules may be impressed upon him
3. Support the principal in encouraging him to seek another location for student teaching
4. Suggest that you meet at a restaurant or some other location for conversation
5. Suggest that you will call him back after the principal leaves and he can then meet you at the school
6. Tell the principal that he is still in town and that you would like to meet with him here in the school building since the pupils have now left
7. _____

Consider:

a. Early communication of school policies and their values
b. The effect of the incident upon successful inauguration of student teaching
c. Your own attitudes concerning appearance
d. _____

ASSOCIATING WITH MEMBERS OF THE OPPOSITE SEX: **A Date with Doom**

Student teachers in secondary schools are aware of the narrow age span between them and their pupils. This can be quite apparent in contacts with members of the opposite sex. The male student teacher can easily find himself to be the target of the affection of some of his female students. A female student teacher may observe that some of the older boys are attracted to her and that they exercise some rather exasperating techniques in attempting to secure her attention.

Problems occur when the student teacher makes incorrect reactions to the overtures of the students. The male student teacher may be flattered by the attention of a high school girl and arrange to find time to be with her during the school day or to be alone with her in school-related activities. Taking her home after an evening meeting seems not only logical but decent. Sometimes he may find himself in difficulty for merely sitting next to a girl on a bus which transports pupils to a game or contest. The student teacher who is immature or unaware may arrange social engagements such as dates. He may gravitate more and more to the company of this student because she will probably offer support and warmth when response from the tasks of student teaching may lead to more uncomfortable feelings. The problems will develop as he begins to lose the respect of the pupils and acquire the wrath of an administration which subscribes to complete separation of faculty and pupils in regard to informal social relationships.

A girl may find that one or more of the boys in her class may be annoying her. The male attraction to the female student teacher will more likely follow a different style. A student teacher may find that a boy is following her around all the time or annoying her in class instead of initiating contacts which suggest dating. She perceives the relationship to be a discipline problem and generally responds accordingly. She will probably be somewhat reluctant to accept the suggestion that the boy's behavior is caused by a "crush" on her.

Occasionally, supervising teachers may have to intervene to save the student teaching experience. Several alternatives are available in considering an appropriate course of action in such a situation:

Explain to the student teacher why certain pupils are reacting as they are

See that the problem is discussed early so that he may see the possible ramifications of too much informality with certain members of the opposite sex

Alert him to situations in which his actions could be considered impertinent

If he is participating in activities which are conducive to informal contact, attempt to be present or arrange it so that he inadvertently will not be placed in an embarrassing position

Talk to the pupils involved and solicit their cooperation

Suggest methods which the student teacher can utilize in maintaining the traditional teacher-pupil relationship

Case Study No. 72: YOUR STUDENT TEACHER TAKES A PUPIL TO A COLLEGE DANCE

Your student teacher obviously was enjoying the attention of Vicki, a precocious senior who was attracted to this new male in the classroom. No problems seemed to exist until one Monday morning when Vicki announced that she had been to a college dance with your student teacher and that they "had a ball." You had no advance knowledge that your student teacher and Vicki were involved in a social relationship. You sense the problem when he walks down the hall and several of the pupils make comments about the "swinging week-end." He greets you without any comment. What do you do?

1. Make no reference to it until it is openly brought to your attention
2. Indicate that you know what has happened and describe for him what repercussions are bound to follow
3. Let events develop naturally and assist him in interpreting the results of this action
4. Talk to the girl and explain the student teacher's new problem

5. Ask that his student teaching be terminated _____
6. _____

   Consider:

   a. Immediate effect upon the classroom environment
   b. Procedures which can help him re-establish himself
   c. Means of preventing future occurrences which might prove damaging to the class or the student teacher
   d. _____

Case Study No. 73: THE FEMALE STUDENT TEACHER IS AN-NOYED BY A HIGH SCHOOL BOY

   Lana likes most of the pupils she teaches, but she complains that John is quite annoying to her. She says that he follows her around and keeps asking her questions or making comments about nearly everything. In class he is always talking or creating a disturbance of some sort. She asks for your help. What do you do?

1. Explain that he probably is very fond of her and suggest that she show some affection which will cause him to be embarrassed and avoid her
2. Talk with the pupil and ask him to alter his behavior
3. Suggest she avoid him by appearing to be busy or by taking different routes so that he cannot intercept her so easily
4. Tell her to be more firm in dealing with him
5. Ask her to talk with the pupil and explain how difficult it is for her to teach with his acting as he does
6. _____

   Consider:

   a. Whether the student teacher will accept the notion that the boy displays affections toward her
   b. The effect upon the pupil
   c. Whether it would be more effective for teacher or student teacher to attempt to eliminate the problem
   d. _____

   The discussion of problems at the conference had been rather depressing to Miss Bennett initially, but then she began to realize that this open treatment would probably be of benefit to her if she ever had any such difficulties. She felt better prepared now in the event such a situation should ever happen in her class.
   She returned to her school the next day wondering about Brian's solo experience. "How did it go yesterday?" she quickly asked.
   "Great," replied Brian. "I was an instant success with them since I wore some of my new 'mod' clothes. I demonstrated how to make 'mellow yellow', and I even taught them to sing a couple of protest songs."
   Miss Bennett was temporarily confused until she spied Bill Larson, her practical-joker associate from across the hall, who had attended the group

meeting with her. His innocent face immediately told the story. She broke into an instant smile, somewhat relieved to know that Bill had gotten to Brian first and tipped him off about the proceedings at the conference. She was inwardly convinced that a lot of problems could be thwarted if the supervising teacher and student teacher can be comfortable enough with each other to inject a little humor into the professional environment.

Remember:

The problem student should be given all possible chance and help to succeed and should not be summarily dismissed as incapable

Thorough communication is a great asset in the prevention of difficulties

Anticipation of a problem and then taking preventive measures is much less complicated than arresting a dilemma once it has developed

Many awkward situations result from incorrect and poorly considered reactions to a set of stimuli

Problems often come to the forefront when success is denied

USEFUL REFERENCES

CURTIS, DWIGHT, AND ANDREWS, L. O., *Guiding Your Student Teacher*, Prentice-Hall, 1954, Chapter 12
    Promoting personal development
STRATEMEYER, FLORENCE B., AND LINDSEY, MARGARET, *Working with Student Teachers*, Teachers College Press, Columbia University, New York, 1958, Chapters 4, 16
    College students as learners
    Guiding your student in the transition from college student to member of the profession

Chapter Eleven

EVALUATING THE STUDENT TEACHER

Brian Sims' performance as a student teacher had exceeded Miss Bennett's hopes. He was pleasant, cooperative, liked by the students, and well grounded in his teaching area. His plans were submitted on time and he seemed to be effective in teaching students at all ability levels. As a result, Miss Bennett felt that she might be doing a disservice to Brian if she delved into a great number of evaluative "critiques."

She began to have some reservations about her decision after the last visit from Dr. Phillips, Brian's college supervisor. He inquired extensively about the amount of time spent in evaluation, whether Brian was beginning to develop the ability to evaluate himself, and how much use they had made of the evaluation checklist in the university guide for student teaching. Her responses were brief and evasive, because she felt that such was not necessary since his progress was quite satisfactory.

Dr. Phillips stressed that the best evaluation occurred when there was frequent analysis of teaching, emphasizing both teaching strengths and attacking teaching problems. Although she did not protest to Dr. Phillips, she felt that such techniques might tend to cause Brian to lose confidence. Still, she resolved that she would discuss this matter with some of the other teachers who had supervised student teachers, and she also intended to ask Brian about his feelings concerning the type of evaluation which he expected . . .

EVALUATION: Judgment Day, Pay Day, or Just Another Day?

Student teaching is designed to provide professional articulation from college student to beginning teacher. Probably no other block of studies demands as much change in so many areas as does the semester in which student teaching is completed. The road to progress is not as clearly marked as it is in the college course work. There are no quizzes, examinations, and term papers to indicate achievement or mastery of subject. Even if there were, they would be shallow procedures in measuring the complex process of student teacher growth. Tangible devices for indicating development come in different forms and require constant attention if they are to be of any value in appraisal.

One of the fundamental concepts of student teaching is that growth is accomplished more efficiently when experience in the classroom is coupled with the appropriate guidance of a more experienced professional. If the experienced professional--the supervising teacher--does not share his insights on teaching and help the student teacher comprehend his own progress in teaching ability, he thwarts the student teacher's progress as much as a plant is thwarted if it does not get the benefit of the rain and sunshine. Indeed, if no directed evaluation is provided by the supervising teacher, there is no justification for a period of student teaching, since unassisted experience is likely to be his plight as a first-year teacher.

The supervising teacher is in the most sensitive position as far as evaluation is concerned. He devotes more time to the student teacher than any other professional, including those at the college or university. He understands the combination of pupils and subject better than any other person connected with a particular student teacher. Therefore, he is best able to determine those moves that are likely to be the most effective. He is the one who is best able to recognize the strengths, problems, and individual characteristics of the student teacher. His continuous task is to help the teaching candidate recognize these components and to formulate techniques of improvement.

Evaluation will have priority in the mind of the student teacher. His immediate concern will likely be the superficial, "How am I doing?" In a broader context, his thoughts will focus on what the people who will submit grades or evaluation reports think of him. A lack of clues or reinforcement concerning evaluation can lead to frustration and anxiety. Evaluation is anticipated, and most student teachers are eager for some indication of their progress.

More important than the occasional "okay" or traumatic "alarm" response is the process of a continuous evaluation. This constant process enables the student teacher and his supervising teacher to team up to analyze performance and to design methods which will help develop a better instructional technique. Analysis of good procedures and strategies can be as valuable as a look at weaker practices, and a discussion of why certain procedures are effective can create as much understanding or improvement as a look at those techniques that need betterment. Therefore, evaluative discussions must not be limited solely to areas of a student teacher's performance that need to be changed, but they should provide review of all aspects of teaching.

The student teacher places a great amount of confidence in the supervising teacher's ability to make accurate appraisals of his teaching. If he does not receive these assessments, he will most likely perform on an "intellectual plateau," showing little or no improvement, and he will become increasingly concerned because the supervising teacher gives no indication of progress.

As vital as he is, the supervising teacher is only involved temporarily in the evaluation procedure. His goal is to eliminate the need of his assistance by developing the student teacher's skill in making valid judgments about his own teaching. Hopefully, this can be achieved by the time the student teacher concludes his experience; realistically it cannot be hoped that it is possible much before this terminal point in student teaching. A considerable amount of time must be devoted to encouraging reflection and to discussing concepts of teaching.

The evaluation procedure, then, is not a checklist of "goods" and "bads." It is an intellectual process involving many "why's" and "how's" embellished by apt and revealing comments from the supervising teacher. In other words, it is not just the final score; it is what the game is all about.

Effective evaluation focuses on concern for the student teacher's progress in particular and the improvement of teaching in general. A detached look at both simultaneously is more likely to bring about acceptance by the one being evaluated. If the student teacher approaches evaluation with the feeling that he and the supervising teacher are working on a problem, he can be more objective than when he perceives that the more experienced person is grading or judging the less experienced apprentice.

Evaluation is more than the determination of a grade or the completion of a checklist, because those acts often do little to clarify the obscurity which either of them can provide about the actual ability of the student teacher. Evaluation is not a report; it is a process which is interwoven in the entire experience of a student teacher. This continuous procedure makes the following principles apparent for the student teacher and those concerned with his progress:

The process of evaluation should be designed to prepare the student teacher to evaluate himself objectively and with a valid frame of reference

Evaluation should make apparent those skills and techniques which are essential for good performance as a teacher

Evaluation should identify specific areas that need improvement as well as recognize those that are of good quality

Evaluation should provide guidelines for the next steps in learning about teaching

Evaluation should furnish an objective description of the student teacher's ability and potential for teaching to a prospective employer

A successful student teaching experience should prepare a teaching candidate to perform at a level that is consistent with minimum professional standards. The supervising teacher will be responsible for assisting in the achievement of that level of proficiency which will qualify the student teacher for entrance into the teaching profession.

Most teacher education institutions rely heavily upon the supervising teacher's judgment in determining whether to recommend the candidate for a teaching credential. Within a relatively brief period of time, levels of competence must be assessed in regard to the teaching performances listed below. The supervising teacher should be aware of them in assessing progress and in structuring the working environment of a student teacher.

The ability to manage a classroom independently
    A teacher should be capable of performing the various tasks
    of teaching without depending upon another person

A teacher should be capable of making his own professional decisions from the knowledge he has acquired

The ability to objectively appraise his own teaching

Human relations with pupils, teachers, and other professional personnel associated with the school

Academic background

Teaching skills such as planning, organizing ideas, communication of ideas, and encouraging thinking

The ability to structure the classroom environment so that learning can occur

Pupils display evidence of acquisition of knowledge

Pupils demonstrate evidence of skill development

Pupils' performance indicates that objectives are being met

The ability to understand the purpose of a school and the role of a teacher in that institution

Philosophy and goals of the school

The activities and processes which contribute to learning

The activities and responsibilities of a teacher

The ability to establish desirable and effective relationships with students, teachers, administrators, and parents

Adjust effectively to conditions of stress that can result from such working relationships

Provide the type of professional leadership needed to affect others positively

The ability to identify, develop, and execute positively those characteristics which are recognized as teaching skills

An understanding of the conditions under which individuals learn and the facility to alter conditions to gain desired learning

The ability to structure the learning environment so that desirable changes in pupil performance can be produced

The ability to develop effective instruments which will measure the degree of behavioral change or skill development

Case Study No. 74: THE STUDENT TEACHER FEELS THAT SHE IS RECEIVING TOO MUCH CRITICISM

You are cognizant of the various capabilities necessary for good teaching, and you are just as aware that student teaching offers a relatively brief period of time for the development of these traits. Unfortunately, your student teacher is going to need all the help she can get. So, you have been working very intensely in helping her perform better. The full impact of your efforts is realized after a long conference dealing with problems and she inquires, "Am I doing anything right?" What do you do?

1. Recognize that she is, but that you are attempting to help her use more techniques correctly
2. Re-examine your concept of evaluation and spend some time discussing in detail those procedures that are successful
3. Ask her what she thinks
4. Indicate that your comments are not personal but are designed to focus on the action of improving teaching in general
5. Indicate that when she shows evidence of self-evaluation, you will not have to provide as much input
6. ――――――――――――――――――――――――――――――

Consider:

a. The broad concept of evaluation of student teaching
b. Processes in helping a student teacher become self-directive
c. The type of changed evaluative procedure that student teaching has in comparison to college course work
d. ――――――――――――――――――――――――

GUIDELINES FOR THE EVALUATIVE PROCESS: **Studying the Rules**

Evaluation must begin with some frame of reference. Effective growth cannot take place if comment is only made in regard to overall effectiveness or through vague statements relating to the student teacher's skill or progress. Comments such as "you are doing all right" convey little real support or information. Furthermore, such vague remarks give no direction for improvement of teaching.

Any evaluation of teaching is based on a concept of what constitutes good teaching. A decision concerning a superficial or an in-depth approach depends on how thoroughly the individual actually understands what is involved in teaching. In evaluation, the supervising teacher will not only convey his concept, but that belief very well may be accepted as valid by the student teacher who will then develop his teaching around that set of values. The effective supervising teacher will have analyzed his philosophy of teaching so that he may develop a more comprehensive outlook in his own understanding and in his communication with the student teacher.

In its yearbook on evaluation of student teaching,[1] the Association for Student Teaching identified eleven principles of evaluation. These principles can help formulate a general concept for sophisticated appraisal:

1. The evaluation of student teaching must be based upon and function with a democratic philosophy of education

1 Association for Student Teaching, **Evaluating Student Teaching,** 1960, Chapter 2.

2. The evaluation of student teaching should be made within a behavioral frame of reference
3. In evaluating student teaching the objectives should be defined and stated in terms of the kinds of behavior expected to be realized
4. The methods, procedures, and techniques used in appraising the work of the student teacher should be sufficiently diagnostic to enable the student teacher to identify the various stages of growth and progress involved in learning to teach
5. Evaluation of student teaching should be conceived as an integral part of all learning, to be engaged in cooperatively by the student teacher, the supervising teacher, and the pupils
6. The evaluation of student teaching should lead to a better understanding of growth and development and its relationship to developmental tasks and learning
7. The evaluation of the student teacher's performance should lead to a more realistic understanding and acceptance of "self" and to the development of a positive emotional approach to teaching, learning, and living
8. The evaluation of the student teacher can be educative only to the extent that it recognizes and reconstructs the group experiences which the student teacher brings with him to the student teaching situation
9. The evaluation of student teaching is broader than measurement and requires the use of both quantitative and qualitative data
10. The mere description of the characteristics of a "good teacher" is insufficient for evaluating teacher competencies needed in a democratic social order
11. The evaluation of student teaching is comprehensive, continuous, and leads to improvement in the total program of teacher education

Evaluation involves a great deal more than what is normally conceived by the average supervisor. It includes an awareness of what should be done as well as the procedure of effecting change toward that goal. Several moves are helpful in the creation of a favorable environment for evaluation. The following present a picture of the challenges which should be met for an effective process:

Offer suggestions for improvement or reinforcement of technique as soon after the experience as possible
Evaluation should focus on the activity instead of the person
    Why did the class go as it did?
    Why did the class go well?

What was difficult about this lesson?
Why did the students become restless near the end?
What was learned from the group discussion?
What caused the problem?

Suggestions for improvement should be positive whenever possible

*Ask questions of the student teacher instead of merely listing good and
weak points*

Use a variety of evaluative procedures and techniques

Evaluation should be specific

Specific ideas can be implemented more readily than generalizations

Evaluation should be individualized

No two student teachers have the same needs or progress at
the same rate

Many factors demand frequent attention in the evaluation process. Some will likely be stressed by the university. Others may become apparent on an incidental basis during student teaching. The alert supervising teacher will develop an awareness of various components of teaching and be prepared to discuss them with his student teacher. Many of the important skills can be subsumed into the following three areas:

Personal Qualities
Appearance
Physical health and vitality
Poise
Sense of humor
Voice
Interpersonal relationships
Dependability
Judgment
Use of English

Professional Qualifications
Knowledge of professional education
Commitment to teaching
Professional spirit
Attitude toward children

Teaching Skills
Knowledge of subject
Handling of routine procedures
Planning and preparation of materials
Evaluation of pupil achievement
Provision for individual differences
Classroom management
Teacher-pupil relationships

Conduct of class discussions
Supervision of study

Case Study No. 75: THE SUPERVISING TEACHER FAILS TO RECOGNIZE SUCCESSFUL PERFORMANCE

You had a feeling of real satisfaction about your student teacher's progress. She was meeting her responsibilities and was making effective classroom presentations. Since she was performing well you saw nothing to criticize and felt that constant praise might prove embarrassing to her. You are concerned though when you inadvertently learn that your student teacher has been disturbed because you were not evaluating her, and she has been worrying about what she is doing that is so bad that you will not discuss it with her. She indicated that you had made no comments about her teaching for two weeks. You pass by unnoticed, but you resolve that you will re-establish communication with her. What do you decide to do?

1. Explain to your student teacher that you feel that her teaching is satisfactory
2. Adopt a system where you concentrate on only one specific factor or quality at a time
3. Review an evaluation form with the student teacher so that she will have a tangible appraisal of her performance
4. Indicate that you will concentrate on problems and will make such comments when you think they are necessary

5. —————————————————————————

Consider:

a. The importance of explaining good traits as well as those which need to be improved
b. The various qualities which should be considered for a thorough process of evaluation
c. —————————————————————————

Case Study No. 76: REACTING TO A PARTICULARLY POOR LESSON

Your student teacher had just completed the poorest lesson that he has taught. He was impatient with pupils, talked too rapidly, and was incorrect in some of the facts presented. Since there are several problems, you will have to establish priorities and determine the best method of procedure. What do you do?

1. Record your various thoughts on paper and let him read your comments
2. Plan an extensive conference session and utilize a set of key questions which are designed to elicit self-appraisal

3. Concentrate on only one area at a time so that some improvement can be observed quickly

4. _____

Consider:

a. The effect of teacher behavior upon pupil learning
b. Methods of relating specific problems to the overall goals of education
c. _____

TECHNIQUES FOR EFFECTIVE EVALUATION: **Choosing the Correct Tool**

A high degree of skill in communication is demanded in evaluation. In the first place, specificity is desired in order to make known exactly how a student teacher is progressing. Secondly, evaluation can be an emotional experience and an ill-chosen word or phrase can create moods which were unintended or which are detrimental to relationships with the student teacher. Furthermore, if effective communication does not occur, the student teacher is left without the benefit of the teacher's insights.

The type of technique will vary with the task, the student teacher, the supervising teacher, and available time. A student teacher who is open can probably be evaluated directly. The tense, insecure student teacher may require a more subtle approach. Some ideas may need to be transmitted specifically through written communication, while others may need to be developed through oral dialogue. Some situations require an experience where the student teacher looks at himself and subsequently develops a profile of his teaching ability with the assistance of the supervising teacher.

Various techniques will be needed, depending upon the individual situation. The supervising teacher will have to decide on the procedure that can be of most value. The following procedures are frequently employed by supervising teachers in the evaluation process:

Evaluation by conference
   Brief discussion of one or two areas of concern
Longer analysis through dialogue or counseling
   In-depth discussions of problems or ideas
Written comments
   Suggestions or observations can be carefully worded for greater clarity or understanding
   Provides an alternate, and sometimes easier, way for the supervising teacher to offer criticism of the student teachers's activities
   May be received more objectively by the student teacher than oral suggestions

Provides a record for future referral
Rating scales and analysis forms
    Judgments may be perceived to be less arbitrary
    Forces consideration of a variety of teaching skills
    Leads to student self-evaluation
Audio tape recordings of a student teaching activity
    Provides opportunity for student to hear himself and ob-
      serve such factors as speech and questioning techniques
Video tape recording of a student teaching activity
    Allows the student teacher to view the activity as well as
      hear it
    Enlarges possibility for understanding

Mid-term Evaluation

The midpoint in student teaching affords a good opportunity for a more comprehensive look at evaluation. The student teacher has been in the school long enough for patterns to emerge, and he has enough time left so that concentrated effort can be expended to further develop teaching techniques. A comprehensive evaluation can be reassuring, both in terms of progress that has been made and in allowing time to improve in areas of weakness.

Some universities require that supervising teachers file mid-term reports. Discussion of those reports can be enlightening for the student teacher, especially if he is allowed to participate in his own evaluation. Such a tangible form of evaluation can also provide a great amount of reassurance for the student teacher, because this may be the first concrete analysis for him.

Evaluation by pupils can be of real significance at this time as well. Instead of waiting until the end to discover pupil reactions, the student teacher can solicit comments while there is still time to improve. Pupils may be more constructive, too, if they know that they are having a real part in improving the classroom environment.

Encouraging Independent Self-Evaluation by the Student Teacher

A periodic independent self-evaluation can create worthwhile reflection on the part of the student teacher in that he can give thoughtful consideration to the question of the type of teacher he is becoming. He can develop considerable insight if he periodically records significant events and prevalent thoughts about his work in the school. Intervals of two to three weeks allow time for new experiences and adjustment to make writing profitable.

The written self-appraisal may be open-ended in order to allow an opportunity for expression of concerns and ideas which are the most predominant. Student teachers who want some guidelines for such writing might begin by responding to the following kinds of considerations:

Human relations
    With pupils
    With teachers
    With others
Academic background
    In his teaching fields
    In related areas
    In general education
Teaching skills
    Making plans
    Organizing ideas and priorities
    Communication skills
    Using materials and resources
    Encouraging thinking
Unique contributions to the school and to the students

The Summary Evaluation

The summary evaluation will likely be a report to the university as far as the form is concerned. As far as the process is concerned, it may be the final opportunity for the supervisor and student teacher to communicate. The student teacher will be vitally interested in knowing what the supervisor has to say because it can well affect the type of position he will secure.

A discussion of the final report can be a rewarding terminal experience for the student teacher provided that there are no last-minute unpleasant surprises. The final report should be a summary of points which have been previously discussed and worked on during the student teaching period. Such a conference can present a profile of the student teacher, indicating his strong points as well as his weaker traits. It can also serve as the time when recommendations may be considered relating to the type of position to pursue, the special skills which should be continued, and procedures for improving those techniques that are not as strong as they could be. The summary evaluation, then, becomes a road map for the future.

Evaluation by Pupils

Pupil evaluations can provide another perspective on the effectiveness of a student teacher's performance in that they reveal the impressions of those he has been attempting to teach. Pupils may be able to make suggestions to the student teacher that the supervising teacher either is not aware of or cannot successfully convey to him. Older pupils, obviously, can be more articulate in their evaluations than the younger children.

The climate of the pupil evaluation is quite important. First of all, a pupil must feel that the student teacher is sincere and will attempt to incorporate the valid suggestions into constructive action. Some student teachers have found that evaluation is more successful if it is projected, i.e., a student teacher asks for suggestions on how one of his particular classes should be taught differently next year so that the present students will not be affected by their statements.

The student teacher's fear of pupil evaluations is one obstacle which will need to be overcome. The inexperienced student teacher may suspect that the pupils will barrage him with harsh or unfair criticisms in an effort to "get even." Other student teachers will be looking for praise only and can be quite concerned if there is even one poor evaluation. Once the student teacher understands the context of pupil evaluations and selects the proper device, he should find that pupils can offer some very constructive evaluations of his work.

There are many different ways of soliciting pupil evaluations. One of the simplest and most popular methods is the administration of pupil rating forms. These forms can be completed quickly and anonymously. They also have the advantage of focusing on the particular concerns desired by the student teacher.

Perhaps the most informative and most revealing pupil evaluations come from open-ended questions such as the following:

What did you like best about the class?
What did you like least about the class?
If your student teacher were to teach this class again, what changes should be made?

The open-ended type of question lets the student express his ideas in his own words. It is less restrictive and permits a pupil to say that which is prevalent in his own thinking. The following comments are written comments made to student teachers as they terminated their student teaching and asked for pupil appraisal:

"I thought you were a very good teacher. In my other classes the teacher makes the whole period dull. I like it when a teacher changes his voice tone and walks around while lecturing. I have learned more this week than all the rest. I understand the chapters much better, too."
"Some tips I get from mother. She helps me at times when I need it. In the last week I didn't need to ask for any help."
"I fully believe that you will make an excellent teacher. You make the

work more interesting and easier to absorb. I've done worse in my classwork, but this is my fault. On one chapter, I think it was Chapter 29, I did learn more and was more interested than I have been all semester. People can feel when a teacher is interested in them. But I think I can be justified to say that the class as a whole has enjoyed having you teach us. We have learned more, and with more interest. What interests me is the way you put in the personal details and facts that make learning an adventure. You have a contagious energy, and this will help in any vocation. But it is needed most in teaching."

STUDENT TEACHERS' REACTIONS TO EVALUATION BY SUPERVISING TEACHERS: Are Your Ears Burning?

The following is a list of evaluative statements concerning supervisory techniques which were solicited from student teachers. Although student teachers react in terms of their own needs or priorities, the statements reveal some of the most prominent concerns regarding techniques of evaluation by supervising teachers:

The teacher corrected me in front of the class. This was very devastating to me.

The teacher never let me know that I had this problem until it was reported on the final evaluation form. I wish I had known sooner so that I could have worked on it.

The teacher just doesn't say anything to me about how I am doing.

The teacher said I was doing all right, but did not indicate what I was doing right or why I was doing all right.

The teacher was very helpful in going over the lesson with me and telling me where I needed improvement.

The teacher never seemed to threaten me in our discussions. He was careful to point out that all of us have areas where improvement is needed.

I always knew where I stood.

Criticism was always combined with praise.

Case Study No. 77: EVALUATING THE STUDENT TEACHER WHO SEEMS TO DO EVERYTHING WELL

Ann is doing so well teaching your classes that you find it difficult to think of her as a student teacher. There seem to be no areas where any type of criticism is warranted. How do you go about establishing any kind of evaluation procedures in this situation?

1. Concentrate on the procedure of discussing why teaching is good

2. Examine your own knowledge of teaching to determine if you are correct in your assessment
3. Attempt to create some problem situations which might extend the student teacher's ability to teach successfully
4. Let the experience proceed naturally
5. _____

Consider:

a. Effect of continuous praise upon a student teacher
b. Effect of no analysis procedures in response to evaluations
c. The concept of what constitutes effective teaching
d. _____

Case Study No. 78: THE PUPIL EVALUATION CREATES CONCERN ON THE PART OF THE STUDENT TEACHER

Your student teacher decided to have his pupils evaluate the class using an open-ended technique. Most of the comments were constructive, but three were very critical. The student teacher was quite upset by these. Although the negative comments were blunt, they did identify a problem or two which the student teacher could seek to alleviate. How do you discuss these negative comments with your student teacher?

1. Call attention to the fact that the vast majority of the class likes his work
2. Attempt to help him to objectively evaluate the criticisms
3. Tell him to ignore the comments as the product of jokers.
4. _____

Consider:

a. Methods of preparing a student teacher for pupil evaluation
b. Possible implications of pupil evaluations upon future performances
c. _____

Case Study No. 79: ESTABLISHING A FRAME OF REFERENCE FOR TEACHING

Before you realize it, the inevitable evaluation form has to be completed. As you peruse the form, you see that some questions are going to have to be reconciled before you can make the appraisal. The source of confusion results when you read a checklist and discover that you have to check several criteria as outstanding, above average, average, or below average. Since you are not certain what degree of excellence is associated with these terms, how do you proceed?

1. Compare your student teacher with other student teachers you may have known
2. Compare your student teacher with first year teachers of your acquaintance
3. Formulate concepts for the terms and rate accordingly
4. Forget about the possible definitions of the terms and produce a profile which identifies strong, average, and weak areas of performance
5. Contact the college supervisor and seek his interpretation
6. _____

Consider:

a. The ultimate impact of the evaluation
b. The implications of comparison with other individuals
c. The information which a reader of this appraisal would want to know
d. _____

Case Study No. 80: DECIDING HOW TO PROVIDE INCREASED EVALUATIVE INPUT TO A RELUCTANT STUDENT TEACHER

You made a few early evaluative comments which appeared to disturb the student teacher. After this, he seemed to avoid evaluation and you did not make a point of criticizing because of his reactions. You realize that you soon will have to provide more evaluative assistance in spite of his objections. Otherwise, he will remain on an intellectual plateau and complete student teaching without a realistic concept of his abilities. How do you re-establish communication?

1. Discuss the matter with the student teacher and explain why continuous evaluation is necessary
2. Return to the procedure of offering periodic evaluation without explanation
3. Return to the procedure of offering periodic evaluation but attempt to utilize a more indirect procedure
4. _____

Consider:

a. The human factor
b. Techniques of helping without appearing to be critical
c. The necessity of continuous evaluation
d. Procedures of evaluation which can be acceptable to both parties
e. _____

Miss Bennett and Brian sat down to consider the evaluation report that she would send to the university for his record. It would be the last formal evaluative session, and both were relaxed and confident as they talked.

Miss Bennett began, "Brian, I think you have excellent potential, and I would be more than pleased to have you work here in Central City if there is a position available. You have a good command of yourself as far as poise is concerned and are superior in establishing student rapport. You are certainly better than average in subject knowledge, use of voice, and creativity. Most of your weaknesses are in the areas of organization and in fostering more real thinking in the classroom discussions instead of seeking recall of facts. However, you showed improvement and will correct these difficulties as you gain experience. None are serious enough to cause any concern for remedial action, of course."

Brian agreed, "I want to work on the techniques of questioning, and I must realize that these students are not as well informed as they sometimes appear. Organization has been a real problem for me, but I realize now how important it is for teaching. I agree with your analysis and would suggest that, if anything, you are too kind. I appreciate all the help you have given me in reaching this point in my professional development."

Remember:

The goal in evaluation is skill in self-evaluation

The conference is the core of the evaluative process

There is no one correct method of evaluating student teachers; the technique is relative to the situation

Identification of good and bad traits should be accompanied by an explanation of why they are considered good or poor

Evaluation should begin when the student teacher starts teaching and continue during the entire period of time

Evaluation is more than passing judgment; it is a process of honest, considerate interaction between two adults

If a supervisor withholds his views concerning a student teacher's progress, the student teacher will usually interpret the silence as criticism

When communication is absent, evaluation is merely condemnation

The student teaching experience presents the final opportunity for teacher appraisal by a person who can observe performance over a sustained period of time

USEFUL REFERENCES

ASSOCIATION FOR STUDENT TEACHING, *Evaluating Student Teaching*, Association for Student Teaching Thirty-ninth Yearbook, 1960
   Principles of evaluating student teachers
   Case reports of institutional practices in evaluating student teaching

BJERSTEDT, AKE, "Interaction--Orientated Approaches to the Assessment of Student Teachers," *The Journal of Teacher Education* 18:339-359, Fall, 1967

CURTIS, DWIGHT K., AND ANDREWS, L. O., *Guiding Your Student Teacher*, Prentice-Hall, 1954, Chapter 13
   Purposes of evaluation

The evaluation program
Use of procedures and materials
Special problems in evaluation

DEVOR, JOHN W., *The Experience of Student Teaching,* Macmillan Co., 1964, Chapter 12
  Evaluating your student teaching experiences

GROVE, THOMAS H., "Improving Student Teacher Performance," *Improving College and University Teaching* 13:246-247, Autumn, 1965

JORDAN, ARCHIE C., "Improving Student Teacher Evaluation," *Peabody Journal of Education* 45:139-142, November, 1967

McCABE, GEORGE E., "Evaluation Atmosphere: Evil or Asset?" *The Journal of Teacher Education* 12:262-270, September, 1961

MEYER, JOHN, AND QUICK, ALAN F., "Let's Do Away With Letter Grades in Student Teaching," *Supervisors Quarterly* 6:1, pp. 11-15, Autumn, 1970

MYERS, GEORGE R., AND WALSH, WILLIAM J., *Student Teaching and Internship in Today's Secondary Schools,* Charles Merrill, 1965, Chapter 8
  Evaluation as a means of promoting growth

SELAKOVICH, DAN, "Self-Evaluation by Student Teachers," *The Journal of Teacher Education* 12:225-228, June, 1961

SLEEPER, WILLIAM R., AND TELFER, HAROLD E., "Evaluation: The Heart of Student Teaching," *The Journal of Teacher Education* 11:71-74, March, 1960
  Evaluative conferences
  Self-evaluation by student teachers
  The final evaluation

STRATEMEYER, FLORENCE, AND LINDSEY, MARGARET, *Working With Student Teachers,* Teachers College Press, Columbia University, New York, 1958, Chapter 15
  Basic principles of evaluation
  Functions of evaluation in student teaching
  Gathering evidence on which to base evaluation
  Interpreting and reporting the student teacher's progress
  Persons who share responsibility for evaluating student teacher growth

TANRUTHER, EDGAR M., *Clinical Experiences in Teaching for the Student Teacher or Intern,* Dodd, Mead, and Co., 1967, Chapter 10
  Evaluating growth in teaching skill

SUMMARY

Brian Sims concluded his last class as a student teacher and bade his pupils farewell. He was unprepared for the emotional reactions of some of his students on this final day, and he was visibly touched by their expressions of regret that he was leaving. The period of student teaching seemed to pass in an unbelievably brief amount of time as far as he was concerned. He conveyed his final appreciation to Miss Bennett and the other school personnel, vowing that he would keep them informed of his future activities. He walked out of Central School as a confident, pleased young professional who liked teaching and was eager to accept a position. As he exited through the doors on his way to his car, he realized that he was a much different person than the insecure young man who timidly walked into the building a few weeks ago. At this moment he was convinced that this experience had exercised a more profound impact on him than any other block of academic and professional study at the university.

Elaine Bennett felt that she was a different person, too. She was certain that she was a better teacher for having had the experience of sharing her classroom with a student teacher. She had reflected more about her own teaching during the past few weeks than she ever had, and she certainly had learned much from Brian as they worked together on mutual teaching activities. Her professional background had been enriched, also, due to the university contacts which had been initiated by this activity. Most of all she felt that the presence of two professionals in the classroom caused her students to receive more attention. She may have helped shape the destiny of a young teacher, but she had also refined her own teaching technique. She allowed herself a final look down the hall as Brian disappeared into a crowd of students and then turned back into her classroom where she gazed for a moment at his empty desk . . .

BECOMING A SUPERVISOR: We Would Rather You Do It Yourself

Brian Sims is the composite of many student teachers and Elaine Bennett is his counterpart in the ranks of the beginning supervisors. Both were as typical as they could be in representing what can be accomplished in an experience where no two situations or people can be exactly alike. Brian's problems and achievements were the ordinary ones, and Miss Bennett made the moves the profession would usually consider to be appropriate. Their example suggests that a teacher and student teacher who are aware of their roles and oriented to their responsibilities can bring about decisive changes in teaching technique.

The content of the book was designed to broaden the professional conceptions of teachers and student teachers rather than prescribe specific techniques which are to be automatically implemented. A teacher is a decision-maker. This is one major characteristic which sets him apart from non-professional positions. The professional teacher has to make decisions from alternatives rather than deploy a pat response from situations which may overtly appear similar. His judgments are based on his awareness of the dynamics of a given situation, the personalities of the people involved, and his own knowledge of practices and their potential effects. The inevitable outcome of his decision-making is manifest by the behavior of those whom he directs. The individuals who came under his influence are now making our laws, manufacturing merchandise and selling it to us, living happy lives, making and breaking homes, snatching purses on the street, erecting buildings, hooked on drugs, and guiding our children. The teacher is not the sole person responsible for molding our society, but there is at least one moment when he can touch another person in such a way that his life will be changed. One such opportunity for cooperating teachers is presented in the student teaching experience.

This book hopefully has expanded the teacher's concepts of options and techniques in guiding student teachers. The pages and chapters have been designed to increase the number of available procedures which a teacher might utilize in making decisions concerning the development of a future teacher. Within a given context virtually any statement or procedure suggested in this book can be right, wrong, or irrelevant. The teacher must consider the entire syndrome of factors and then decide upon an appropriate course of action. The more he knows about the field, the better the possibility that he will make a sound judgment.

A television commercial a few years ago presented an aggravated and irritated lady shrieking, "I would rather do it myself!" In a more reasoned and considered manner, the supervising teacher has to supervise student teachers himself. Other teachers can offer advice, and materials can provide background for making a judgment, but ultimately the decision must be made by the supervising teacher. He must determine a student teacher's basic course because he is the only one who can do it. Instead of a pain pill, his elixir is a combination of knowledge and values which he employs in a professional situation. If he puts them together in the correct manner, his influence will provide the most significant input in a program of teacher preparation.